J. S. Mills

Mission work in Sierra Leona, West Africa

J. S. Mills

Mission work in Sierra Leona, West Africa

ISBN/EAN: 9783743364745

Manufactured in Europe, USA, Canada, Australia, Japa

Cover: Foto ©ninafisch / pixelio.de

Manufactured and distributed by brebook publishing software (www.brebook.com)

J. S. Mills

Mission work in Sierra Leona, West Africa

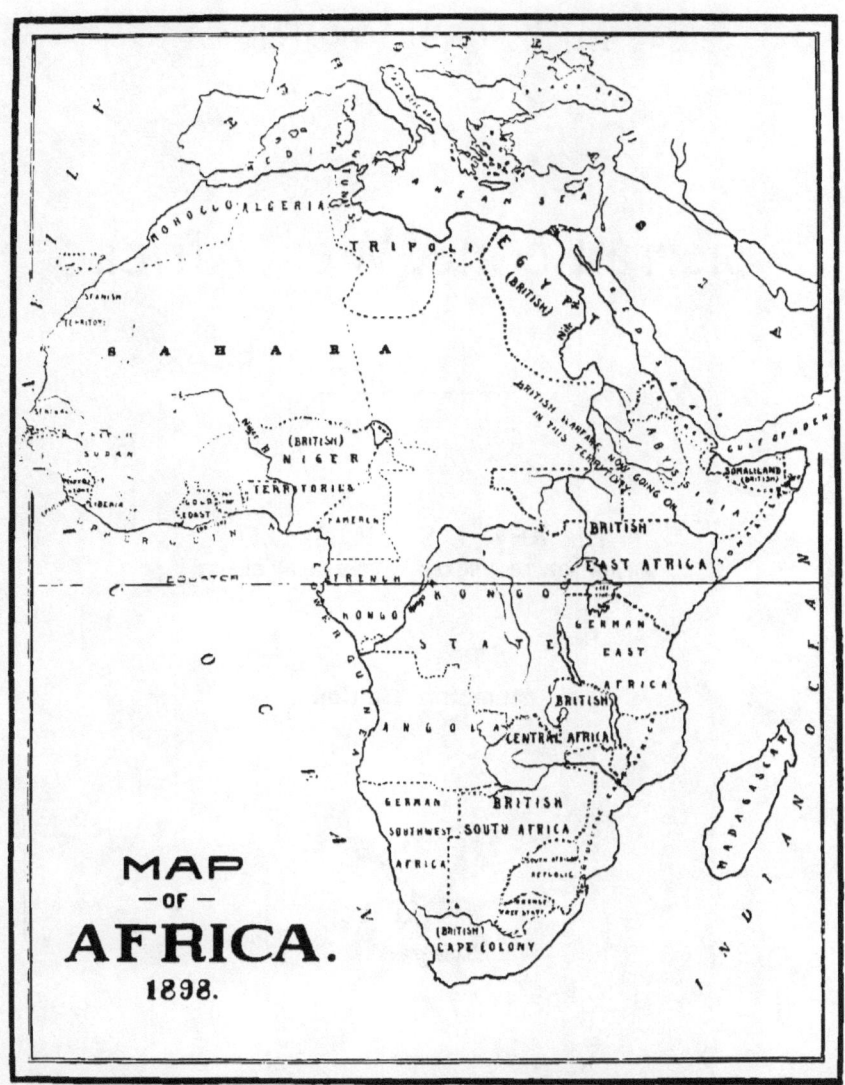

MISSION WORK

IN

Sierra Leone, West Africa

BY

THE REV. J. S. MILLS, D.D
BISHOP OF THE UNITED BRETHREN IN CHRIST

Memorial Edition

DAYTON, OHIO
UNITED BRETHREN PUBLISHING HOUSE
1898

This Book is Dedicated
to the
Memory of Our Heroic Dead
Who lie sleeping in Afric's sunny land;
and to those who will take up and
carry forward the work so
nobly begun.

PREFACE

For over forty years a band of devoted men and women have been toiling in an obscure field on the west coast of Africa. In their schools they have trained for usefulness several hundred of the youth, and have gathered over six thousand converts into native churches.

Early in May, 1898, a heathen mob, displeased at the rapid progress of Christian civilization, and angry over the just requirements of the British Government, swept like a fierce hurricane over this mission field and the surrounding country, murdering seven American missionaries, many native pastors, and several hundred converts, and burning the mission property.

This little volume tells the story by those personally familiar with it. It also gives assurance that neither the burning fevers of the climate nor the blazing fagots and fiercer fury of the "war boys" shall prevent our completing the divinely appointed task in Sierra Leone. Rather will this baptism of fire and blood lead our people to a nobler consecration, and prepare the way among the heathen for a more fruitful harvest to be gathered into the Master's garner.

As I have passed through these pages I have lived over again happy days spent in this mission field. Once more, I have enjoyed the courtesies of the gentlemanly British officers—in the governor's palace and in the police captain's mud hut—so refreshing in this dark land; again, I have renewed the joys of the glorious friendships of this heroic band of missionaries, American and native, all dear to me as my own kindred. If the work shall awaken a greater interest in Africa, and help to send the gospel to its perishing people, this is the only reward I ask: all the profits accruing from the sale of this book are devoted to the mission-work of which it treats.

In the spelling of African names I have tried to follow the example of the British government, believing that this will soon become standard for English-speaking people.

In the making of this book I have done little more than furnish the thread upon which the beautiful pearls of thoughts and sentiments of others are strung. All its defects are mine, all its good qualities are theirs.

For the beautiful style in which it is issued I am indebted to the taste and enterprise of the Manager of the United Brethren Publishing House; and for the reading of the proof and the preparation of the table of contents I am under obligations to the proof-readers of the same house.

J. S. MILLS.

DENVER, COLO., August 1, 1898.

TABLE OF CONTENTS.

	PAGE.
PREFACE	V

PART I.

AFRICA IN GENERAL, AND SIERRA LEONE IN PARTICULAR.

CHAPTER I.

1. PHYSICAL GEOGRAPHY—Location of Africa, Size, Relief, Rivers and Lakes, Climate, Flora, Fauna, Minerals.. 13–19
2. POLITICAL GEOGRAPHY—Berlin Conference, Possessions of the French, the English, Germany, the Congo Free State, Portugal, Italy, Spain, Morocco.. 19–23
3. NATIVE AFRICANS—Races, Languages, the Hamitic Family, Semitic Family, Fulah and Nuba Groups, Negro Systems, the Bantu Family, Hottentots and Bushmen, Religions.................................... 24–30
4. AFRICA'S SIX GREAT CURSES—Paganism, Mohammedanism, Polygamy, War, Rum, Slavery............ 30–35
5. MISSION WORK IN AFRICA—The Bible................. 35–36

CHAPTER II.

1. SIERRA LEONE IN GENERAL—Sierra Leone, Freetown, the Peninsula, Manner of Life, Carrying Trade, Animals, Flora, Protectorate of Sierra Leone, Educational Institutions................................. 37–43
2. SIERRA LEONE TRIBES—Colony Proper, Freetown, Military Road, Bethany Cottage, Sherbros, Bulloms, Lokkohs, Susus, Limbas, Kurankoes, Temni, Mendi, Kroomen....................................... 43–51
3. NATIVE SOCIETY, LANGUAGES, CUSTOMS—Society, Languages, Domestic Customs, Marriage Relations, Dress, Names of Children, Houses, Towns, Religious Customs, Gods, Spirits, Survival of the Soul, Witchcraft, Legal Customs, Means of Determining Guilt or Innocence, Penalty for Stealing........... 51–67

CONTENTS

	PAGE.
4. MISCELLANEOUS MATTERS—Secret Societies, Money, Dancing, Music, Diseases, Hospitality..............	67-72

CHAPTER III.

OUR MISSIONARY WORK IN SIERRA LEONE—First Steps, American Missionary Association, Lease at Shaingay Secured, History of the Caulkers, Woman's Missionary Association, Mendi Mission Obtained, First Results Discouraging, African Conference Assignments for 1898.................... 73-82

CHAPTER IV.

DIFFICULTIES TO BE MET—Climate, Mode of Travel, Dangers and Difficulties of Missionary Life......... 83-89

CHAPTER V.

MECHANICAL, AGRICULTURAL, AND MEDICAL WORK—Natives' Ease of Learning, Native Farming, Industrial Education Needed, Medical Treatment for the Natives, Sickness and Witches, Sick Abandoned 90-98

CHAPTER VI.

SOME WORK BEING DONE—Home for Girls at Rotufunk, Deplorable Condition of Little Girls, What They are Taught, Clark Training School, Course of Study, Languages and Folk-lore, "De Spider an' de People What Whay dey Walker," Devils, Spirits. 99-112

CHAPTER VII.

THE OPEN DOOR—Preaching of the Word Welcomed in Sierra Leone, Few Christian Missionaries, Our Church Unmistakably Led to this Colony.......... 113-119

CHAPTER VIII.

THE MASSACRE—Mutterings of Discontent, Sierra Leone Wars, Causes of the Uprising, the Porroh, Protectorate Established, Plan of Attack, Implements of War, Situation at Shaingay, Bonthe, Avery, Other Stations, Rotufunk, What of the Future, Our Martyred Friends....................................... 120-184

CONTENTS

PART II.

MEMOIRS OF OUR HEROIC DEAD IN SIERRA LEONE, WEST AFRICA.

	PAGE.
LIST OF OUR MARTYRS IN THE MISSIONARY CAUSE	137
ISAAC NEWTON CAIN. Personal Impressions, by Alfred T. Howard	138
MARY ELIZABETH MUTCH CAIN. By Uncle Stewart Forbes	144
MARY C. ARCHER. By Rev. Byron J. Clark	150
MARIETTA HATFIELD. By Rev. Z. T. Hatfield	153
ELLA SCHENCK	162
LOWRY A. AND CLARA B. MCGREW. By Rev. W. L. Bunger and G. A. Funkhouser, D.D. Personal Reminiscences of the Author	166
RECOLLECTIONS. By Mrs. Lida M. West	171
TRIBUTE OF REV. J. R. KING	178
REV. RICHARD N. WEST AND HIS WORK IN AFRICA. By Rev. Isaac N. Cain	180
FRANCES WILLIAMS. By Mary Nense Keister	186
ELMA BITTLE. By Mary Bittle	203
LETTER FROM A MISSION BOY	219
LETTER FROM A MISSION GIRL	220
JOSEPH GOMER. By Rev. William McKee, D.D.	221

APPENDIX.

APPENDIX—Journey through the Mendi Country, Preservation of Health in the Tropics, Books of Reference, Missionaries, and Terms of Service of Parent and Woman's Board	233–240

PART I

AFRICA IN GENERAL AND SIERRA LEONE IN PARTICULAR

PART I

AFRICA IN GENERAL AND SIERRA LEONE IN PARTICULAR

CHAPTER I.

1. PHYSICAL GEOGRAPHY.

Location of Africa. Africa lies south of Europe and southwest of Asia. It is connected with Asia by a narrow piece of land lying south of the east end of the Mediterranean Sea, but since the Suez Canal cuts through this isthmus it may be said to be entirely surrounded by water—the Mediterranean Sea on the north; the Suez Canal, Red Sea, Gulf of Aden, and Indian Ocean on the east; and the Atlantic Ocean on the south and west. The equator passes through it at an almost equal distance from its northern and southern ends.

This continent extends about thirty-five degrees south and thirty-seven north of the equator, and because of its location, in its lowlands and deserts it is the hottest continent on our globe.

Size. Africa is seventy-two degrees (about five thousand miles) long from Cape Bon in the north to Cape Agulhas in the south; and from Cape Guardafui in the east to Cape Verde in the west, it is almost sixty-eight degrees (four thousand and six hundred miles) wide. Its outline is very irregular. It has few islands, except the Madeira, and Canaries, and the Cape Verde islands off the northwest coast, and Madagascar Island off the southeast coast. Africa is almost as large as North America and Europe combined, containing over eleven million five hundred thousand square miles.

Relief. Africa maintains, as a continent, a uniformly high level. Its average height is second only to that of Asia. Nowhere do we see extensive plains raised only slightly above the level of the sea, such as the vast plains of northern Asia, or of the Amazon Valley in South America.

"Almost everywhere, on penetrating inland from the coast, a steep ascent is soon reached, leading either over mountain ranges parallel to the coast, or up a series of terraced escarpments to a high plateau which fills up the greater part of the interior. It is only where rivers have worn channels for themselves through the higher ground that the lowlands stretch any distance inland. On this account Africa has been likened to an inverted saucer, though this comparison holds good rather for the southern half of the continent than as a whole."—*Thornton.*

"Africa, generally speaking, is a vast, ill-formed triangle. It has no peninsulas; it has almost no islands, or bays, or fiords, but three great inlets, three mighty rivers, piercing it to the very heart, have been allocated by a kind nature one to each of its solid sides. On the north is the river of the past, flowing through Egypt, as Leigh Hunt says, 'like some grave, mighty thought threading a dream'; on the west the river of the future, the not less mysterious Congo; and on the east the little-known Zambesi.

"The physical features of this great continent are easily grasped. From the coast a low, scorched plain, reeking with malaria, extends inland in unbroken monotony for two or three hundred miles. This is succeeded by mountains slowly rising into a plateau some two or three thousand feet high, and this, at some hundreds of miles distance, forms the pedestal for a second plateau, four to five thousand feet high, which may be said to occupy the whole of central Africa. It is only on the large scale, however, that these are to be reckoned plateaus at all. When one is upon them he sees nothing but mountains and valleys and plains of the ordinary type covered for the most part with forest."—*Drummond*.

Rivers and Lakes. The great lake region of Africa is found about the sources of the Nile and south and west of these. This region may be compared to the Great Lake region of North America, except that these African lakes have three outlets to the sea instead of one, as in the case of our lakes. Lake Victoria, Lake Albert, Lake Albert Edward, and a few lesser lakes pour their waters through the Nile, running northward into the Mediterranean Sea. Lake Tanganyika, Lake Bangweolo, and Lake Moero empty their waters through the Congo into the Atlantic Ocean, while the Zambesi drains Lake Nyassa into the Indian Ocean. The other most important lakes are Leopold, in the east side of Congo State, and Lake Chad, in the center of the Sudan country. Apart from the rivers along the coast lowlands, the Nile is in the east, rising in the great lake region, flowing north into the Mediterranean Sea, and is in many respects the greatest and most interesting river in the world. The Niger is in the west, and flows in a half circle into the Gulf of Guinea, draining the western part of the Sudan. Both of these rivers are chiefly north of the equator. The Congo takes its rise in the great lake region, and has its outlet in the Atlantic Ocean. The Zambesi rises on the west side of southern Africa, and flows east into Mozambique Channel. In the extreme southern part are found the Limpopo and Orange rivers.

Climate. The climate of a country is determined by the heat and cold, the drouth and moisture, and the light and darkness of that region. While Africa lies chiefly within the tropics, it has a great variety of temperatures. In the extreme north and south the temperature is so mild that these places are health resorts as delightful as any in Europe. And even within the tropics, except along the coasts or in the sandy deserts, the altitude of the land causes a mild temperature, in some places at times quite cold, some of the mountains in this region being covered with perpetual snow. It is not the excessive heat at any one time, but the constant heat that destroys the health of the white man, even on the west coast.

The rainfall is excessive throughout the tropics, in some places amounting to one hundred and fifty inches yearly. In western Africa the rainy season is from the first of May to the last of October; the other part of the year is dry, but the moisture is sufficient during the dry season for all purposes. Throughout the tropics the day and the night are about the same length through the year.

The Flora. There is a wide variety in the quantity and the quality of vegetation in Africa. The great forest regions are near the equator, and mostly on the west side of the continent, as in the Congo basin and on the Guinea coast. In other places are found grassy prairies dotted over with trees, as great parks, the underbrush kept burned off by the annual fires, while in still other regions vast grass meadows extend for miles with few trees. These are the favorite grazing places for domestic or wild animals. Some of the most useful plants found wild in Africa are the date-palm, oil-palm, india-rubber trees and vines, the cotton-plant, the indigo-plant, the ginger-plant, the coffee, the cola, and the gum-copal trees. In general, the coast belt is covered with rank, yellow grass, or, as along the streams, with a dense jungle of brush and vines, to which add along the Guinea coast forests of fine trees.

"The mountainous plateaus, both of them, are clothed with endless forests—not grand, umbrageous forests like the forests of South America, not matted jungles like the forests of India, but with thin, rather weak forests, with forests of low trees, whose half-grown trunks and scanty leaves offer no shade from the tropical sun. The indiscriminate praise formerly lavished on tropical vegetation has received many shocks from recent travelers. In Kaffirland, south Africa, I have seen one or two forests fine enough to justify the enthusiasm of the arm-chair word-painters of the tropics; but so far as the central plateau is concerned, the careful judgment of Mr. Alfred Russel Wallace respecting the equatorial belt in general applies almost to this whole area: 'Flowers there are, small and great, in endless variety; but there is no display of flowers, no gorgeous show of flowers in the mass, as when the blazing gorse and heather bloom at home [in Scotland].'"—*Drummond.*

The Fauna. Among the animals found here are the giraffe, the hippopotamus, the elephant, the antelope, the lion, the leopard, hyena, jackal, buffalo, zebra, wild ass, gorilla, the chimpanzee in certain parts, and monkeys everywhere.

Many kinds of reptiles are found, as the crocodile, viper, adder, black-snake, and boa-constrictor. Not only the ostrich, but many other large as well as small birds are found here. Insects are met in great abundance. Among these the locusts are in the north, and the tsetse is the deadly enemy of domestic animals in the south. The scorpion is found everywhere. The ants are numerous. In some forests they throw up earth-heaps, a few rods apart, larger than the Dutch ovens in Pennsylvania, and not unlike these ovens in appearance. In other places a black line of them crosses our path. The black boys always leap these lines with a run and a jump. The unwary traveler who comes onto these ants also leaps, but not for joy, for the bite of these insects is as painful as a bee-sting. The white ant, or termite (or bug-a-bug, as the natives call it), eats up whatever dead wood, leather, or cloth falls in its way. As the earthworm is not found in Africa, Drummond thinks this ant performs the work of the former by stirring up the soil, and thus aiding the growth of vegetation. He regards it also as the vegetable scavenger of that country, eating up the decaying plants, and limbs and trunks of trees. This accounts for the fact that many of the forests are as free from fallen timber as a cultivated orchard, though I have seen in western Africa many a fallen tree with the appearance of having lain there for years.

Minerals. Salt is found in many places, while in others it is so scarce as to command a very high price. Iron is quite abundant on the west coast, and is widely distributed over the continent. Gold is found in great quantities in south Africa, and in paying amounts on the Gold Coast and in the upper Niger Valley. In the southern part of the continent diamonds have been obtained in the recent past in such quantities as to greatly reduce the price of these precious stones.

2. POLITICAL GEOGRAPHY.

The Berlin Conference, in 1884-85, changed the political face of Africa, though the work of dividing it between European nations began shortly before this date. Formerly civilized nations went to this continent for Africans; near the close of this century they have gone there for Africa, and they now control almost the whole of it.

The French have secured the largest area. Its largest piece of territory lies west of a line drawn from the inner angle of the Gulf of Guinea north to Lake Chad, thence to Cape Bon on the Mediterranean, and includes all that vast region, except Morocco and a Spanish territory lying along the coast southeast of the Canary Islands, and a small piece of Portuguese, and another of German territory, also Liberia, and certain British possessions along the west coast. This region includes the greater part of the Sahara Desert, and it will, no doubt, cost more to administer it than all its income for all time to come. A better part of her spoils is French Congo, lying west and north of the Congo and Ubangi rivers, and extending from near the mouth of the Congo River with an irregular west boundary to Lake Chad. This is a very fine country extending into the heart of the continent. Add to these regions a little spot at the west end of the Gulf of Aden, and the Island of Madagascar, and all the possessions of France in Africa aggregate three million three hundred thousand square miles.

England comes next in the extent, but first in the value of her possessions. Beginning in the northeast, England holds a protectorate relation to Egypt. South of Egypt intervenes Abyssinia, and a piece of unannexed country along the upper Nile between Egypt and British East Africa. Somaliland lies along the Gulf of Aden. And the unannexed part along the upper Nile will probably soon be British.

British East Africa lies along the White Nile, and extends from Fashoda south to Lake Victoria, and east to the Indian Ocean, and west into the heart of the continent. It is separated from British Central Africa by German East Africa, and British Central Africa extends south to British South Africa, and the latter extends to the Cape of Good Hope. To these lands add Zanzibar Island. Thus, on the east side of Africa British possessions extend from the Mediterranean Sea to the south end of the continent, with only two gaps, both together less than one thousand miles wide. When she shall have annexed the territory along the Nile between Berber and Fashoda, her control will be sufficiently complete for a railroad and a water line of transportation to be established between the north end and the south end of this great continent. This is within the possibilities of the next twenty-five years. Add to this vast stretch of the best part of Africa the possessions on the west coast,—Gambia, Sierra Leone, Gold Coast, the Niger territory, and Walfish Bay,—and it aggregates two million three hundred thousand square miles. Of this W. T. Stead has recently said: "All Africa that is comfortably habitable by white men is under the British protection. And again, everything in Africa that pays dividends lies within the sphere pegged out for John Bull by his adventurous sons. Wherever in Africa you find land in which white-skinned children can be bred and reared you will find it within the British zone. And wherever there is in Africa any paying property, that also will be found in the same sphere of influence. All of Africa that is habitable [for white men], and all of Africa that pays its way, that is British Africa."

Germany has nine hundred and twenty-five thousand square miles in Africa. German East Africa lies between British East Africa and British Central Africa, and extends from the coast inland to Lake Tanganyika. German Southwest Africa lies between British South Africa and the Atlantic Ocean. Add to these Kamerun, on the west coast, extending from the inner angle of the Gulf of Guinea north to Lake Chad.

The Congo Free State is under the protection of Belgium, and lies in the basin of the Congo River. It has vast possibilities, and contains nine hundred thousand square miles.

Portugal has Angola on the west coast, and this is separated from Portuguese East Africa by British Central and South Africa. When to this is added Portuguese Guinea, on the west coast north of Sierra Leone, the area reaches the sum of seven hundred and fifty thousand square miles.

Italy has a strip of land along the Red Sea, north of Abyssinia, and another along the Indian Ocean, east of Abyssinia, in all about four hundred and twenty thousand square miles. How long she can hold this territory is in doubt; the probabilities are that Abyssinia will soon control a part or all of it.

Spain has about two hundred and fourteen thousand square miles of the west end of the Sahara Desert bordering on the Atlantic Ocean, and the Canary Islands.

Morocco in the north, Abyssinia in the east, the Boer republics in the south, and the territory lying between Egypt and Abyssinia on the east and the French Sahara region on the west, including Tripoli, making about three million square miles in all, are the only parts of Africa not yet annexed by some one of the nations of Europe; but it is morally certain that the portions of this worth occupying will soon be absorbed by England, France, or Germany, except, perhaps, Abyssinia. This partition has in most cases been effected peacefully; but at this time (1898) the relations between England and France are much strained over their boundaries, both in the east and the west part of the continent. Our sympathies are with England, who by conquest, commerce, and missions, is doing more than any other nation to lift up Africa, and help her dusky children to enter upon a process of evolution, the extent of which is known only to Him who has "made of one blood all nations of men for to dwell on all the face of the earth, and hath determined the times before appointed, and the bounds of their habitation."

"In the whole of Africa's nearly twelve million square miles, there are probably not more than one million two hundred thousand whites to one hundred and fifty million (or as others estimate two hundred million) natives. Of the former, seven hundred and fifty thousand are in Africa south of the Zambesi, and over three hundred thousand are in Algeria and Tunis, leaving one hundred and fifty thousand for all the rest of the continent. South Africa is the one section of the continent which may become the home of generations of Europeans, and in this respect England has fared best of all the powers. Of the continent between the tropics, all experience up to the present goes to show that it can never be colonized by white races, but must be developed by the natives under white supervision."—*Keltie.*

3. THE NATIVE AFRICANS.

Races. The people in the north part of the continent are of the Caucasian type, having broad skulls, high, straight noses, thin lips, and hair slightly curled. Those living in central and southern regions are of the Ethiopian, or black type, and have narrow skulls, thick lips, flat noses, wooly hair, high cheek-bones, and projecting jaws. On this continent both of these races have dark skins, but of different shades, from a light brown to an ebony black.

The two main divisions of the northern races are Hamites and Semites. The latter occupy the states bordering on the Mediterranean Sea, except Egypt, also part of Abyssinia. The former occupy the Sahara Desert, the north and the south side of Abyssinia, and Egypt. The black or negro race has two main divisions, known as the Sudanese, or negroes proper, and the Bantu tribes. The former occupy the Sudan, from the equator to about fifteen degrees north, and from the Atlantic Ocean east to the Nile. The latter tribes occupy all the continent south of the equator, and are divided into many branches.

It must not, however, be supposed that these races remain of pure blood and distinct from each other. On the contrary, they are frequently found intermixed, and one may find all of them represented in a single community. All the earliest stages of progress are met here. The Bushmen in the extreme south are savages of the rawest type, preying on whomever or whatever they can destroy. Some branches of the Bantus live wholly by hunting. The Sudanese do some farming and

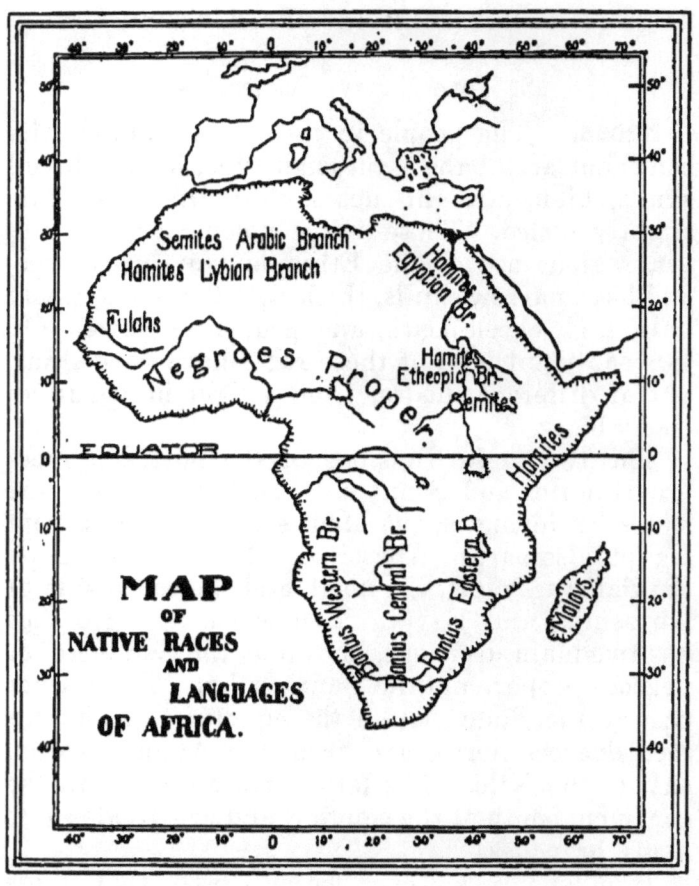

cattle-raising. While the northern races are herders and traders, these and the Sudanese manufacture some articles of clothing from both cotton and goats' hair; also they make a few articles from grasses. A few implements are made of iron, and some ornaments are made of gold, silver, and leather; but, as a rule, the natives are a great "nation of the unemployed." Except along the Nile, their records have perished, if they ever did anything worth recording. They are a vast quantity of raw material, elemental germs, embryonic possibilities, now being brought into contact with the higher races, that the work of redemption and evolution may be accomplished.

Languages. The following description of the native languages is taken from "Africa Waiting," by Thornton:

"1. **The Hamitic Family of Languages** consists of three groups:

"(1) Egyptian, the ancient languages of Egypt and of Moses, with records on stone that date as far back as four thousand years before the Christian era. Under Greco-Christian influences this passed into Coptic, which has survived in ecclesiastical use in the Coptic Church.

"(2) Lybian, or Berber, comprising the indigenous vernaculars of north Africa prior to the Arab invasion, and is still used by the Berbers and Tuaregs. This group undoubtedly presents the ancient languages of Mauretania and Numidia, and later on it was used by Augustine in preaching. It ranks, therefore, among the most venerable of human tongues.

"(3) Ethiopic is strangely intermixed with

other dialects in and around Abyssinia. In this group are found the languages of the Somali and Galla nations in the Eastern Horn, also of the Bisharin, Falashas, and Agau.

"2. **The Semitic Family,** of which there are two branches in Africa:

"(1) The languages of Abyssinia, especially Amharic and Tigre. These are derived from the ancient Geez of southern Arabia, which is still the liturgical language of the Abyssinian Christians.

"(2) Arabic, rightly called one of the conquering languages of the world. 'It is the vehicle of thought over the greater part of Africa, and the instrument of the spread of Islam throughout northern Africa.' Kabyle, Kaffir, and Swahili are Arab names in north, and south, and east, which will long be remembered.

"3. **The Fulah and Nuba Groups,** occupying a position midway between the Hamite and the negro. As Arabic is the language of religion, so *Fulah* is the language of empire. Pure *Nubians* now inhabit the Nile valley, having most likely immigrated from the west between the time of Herodotus and that of Eratosthenes. Both these nations are dominant races, superior in power and culture to lower pagan people. They are also bigoted Moslems.

"4. **The Negro Systems.** The negro and the Bushman probably share the honor of being the original inhabitants of Africa. Certainly the negro type appears distinctly on the monuments of Egypt five thousand years ago. There are three great negro dwelling-places: (1) the western coast, (2) the basin of the Chad, (3) the upper Nile. The pure negro lives, however, in the western half of the Sudan. Their population is estimated at from sixty to a hundred millions, and their distinct languages amount to about two hundred, in addition to innumerable dialects. Among the number of isolated languages, *Hausa* is the most widely spoken, and it is now the commercial language of the whole Sudan. It has several points in common with all the above four groups, and therefore holds a unique position in northern Africa.

"5. **The Bantu Family.** To Dr. Krapf is due the merit of the discovery that a single family of languages prevailed south of the equator throughout Africa. 'The term Bantu is a linguistic rather than an ethnical expression. The now extinct organic Bantu language was of the negro type, but developed along peculiar lines.' Its chief feature consists in the use of prefixes instead of affixes; for example, *aba-ntu aba-kulu,* or 'great men,' as compared with the Latin *fili-a me-a, bon-a et pulchr-a.*

"There are now one hundred and sixty-eight languages and fifty-five dialects, in this family, known by name. They break up into three distinct branches, comprising the Kaffir, Bechuana, and Tekeza branches in the south; the tongues of natives of the Zambesi, Zanzibar, and the great lake regions in the east; and the languages of Angola, the Congo, and the Gaboon in the west.

"6. **The Hottentots and Bushmen.** The great peculiarity of the Hottentot tongue consists in the existence of four clicks, formed by a different position of the tongue, and known as the dental, lateral, guttural, and palatal clicks. Probably these were the original property of the Bushmen, whose speech is monosyllabic, and are thought by some to be the connecting links between articulate and inarticulate sounds. With these are sometimes grouped the pigmy tribes scattered throughout the forest regions of equatorial Africa."

Religions. The nations of Africa profess or observe many religions.

1. Christianity at an early period entered the Dark Continent. At the beginning of the third century it had already been planted in Alexandria and in Carthage. It spread extensively in Egypt and in north Africa, until the beginning of the eighth century, when Mohammedanism, by the power of the sword, spread over these regions, destroying Christianity in the north, but leaving it to linger on in Egypt and Abyssinia. In the former there are still two hundred and fifty thousand, and in the latter over three millions of nominal Christians, but whose environments have led them to a quite imperfect following of Christ.

2. Jewish proselytes were made among the Africans before the beginning of Christianity. There are found to-day over two hundred thousand black Jews in the western part of Abyssinia, the probable descendants of Ethiopian proselytes, and three hundred thousand in Morocco.

3. Mohammedanism, with the exceptions named above, now extends over the whole of north Africa, and into the Sudan to within ten degrees north of the equator. Of course, there are some pagans still living in that region; neither has Islam stopped at the limit named, but it is gradually spreading

southward; some of its followers are already south of the equator.

4. Paganism may be said to be the religion of the natives living south of the tenth degree north of the equator. There are many varieties of this system, but they generally agree in the following points:

(1) One supreme God, under different names, who is rarely worshiped or even referred to. Whether this is their primitive belief, or has been learned from Christians and Mohammedans, is not certain.

(2) The survival of the soul after death is universally believed. The other life is a continuation of the earthly life. Each retains the same rank in the other world he held in this. The cult of the dead consists in the worship of ancestors, of chiefs and deceased sorcerers and priests, and of the spirits who haunt the solitudes of the forests, or who animate nature. This worship is sometimes to appease the anger, and sometimes to gain the good will of the spirits.

(3) The worship of living objects in which these spirits are supposed to dwell. The sacred animals of ancient Egypt have their parallel to-day in the cow, the snake, and other objects of worship.

(4) The fetish is an inanimate object supposed to give its possessor extraordinary power, because a spirit dwells in it. In the form of charms, amulets, or gree-grees of various shapes and substances, this is found everywhere; and it exerts a greater power over the blacks than does their faith in the one God.

(5) Sorcerers, priests, and medicine-men are

generally thought to be possessed by some superior spirit, and are, therefore, greatly feared, but rarely, if ever, loved.

(6) Their religion does not seem to improve their character, and their future lot is not thought to depend on the life they live or the character they form in the present world.

Idols are not universal, but are found in the Congo region and elsewhere.

4. Africa's Six Great Curses.

1. **Paganism** is the worship of false gods, and the religious and social systems growing out of such beliefs and practices. As we have already seen, three-fourths of Africa is under the influence of such customs. The system has permeated all classes; all share its spirit. It is the cry for light of a soul groping in the dark; it is the tendrils of the heart, designed to cling to that which would lift man up into the sunlight, now binding him face downward to the earth; it is the perversion and abuse of man's religious nature, thereby bringing his whole nature into bondage to evil. The wail of despair in the "house of mourning," as well as the beastly orgies in the "devil bush"; the sacrifice of women upon the altar of lust or traffic, as well as the sacrifice of human life upon the altar of heathen gods; the low ideals of their own life, as well as the indifference to the welfare of others, —these and many other sad conditions they owe chiefly to their religious systems. The only remedy is something better to satisfy their spiritual wants and to improve their social state. This is found in the gospel of the Son of God alone.

2. **Mohammedanism.** This system extends over nearly one-third of the continent, has a strong grip on the natives, and, as a whole, is better than paganism. By its fraternal spirit as a sort of freemasonry, its literary language (Arabic), and its monotheistic creed, it has a great power to unify the people and to bind them together wherever it goes. The heathen who adopt it come into fellowship with stronger minds and accept a higher ideal of life. They soon wear better clothes, become more industrious, seek for more knowledge, and where its tenets are obeyed, they live a more sober life. But while it is superior to paganism, it is still a great curse to Africa. It has no power to regenerate the human heart, but on the contrary it encourages polygamy, war, and slavery.

"Sir William Muir, who has studied this question so fully, says very clearly that polygamy, divorce, and slavery are perpetrated and maintained by that religion, striking at the root of public morals, poisoning domestic life, and disorganizing society. Freedom of thought is almost unknown among its adherents, for to abandon Islam is death; therefore it has offered one of the most complete barriers to Christianity. The sword of Mohammed [the jehud] is the most stubborn enemy of liberty, civilization, and truth that the world has ever known."—*Thornton*.

3. **Polygamy** is practiced everywhere in Africa. The women are usually bought of the parents to become the slaves of the men. The woman usually has no choice and no love in her marriage. A man marries as many wives as he can pay for, at about fifteen dollars apiece (in west Africa). Before visit-

ing there, I thought it would be a hardship on the wives to require each man to put away all except one on becoming a member of church; but I am now certain that such an act means liberty to the woman, to be soon followed by a more happy marriage in most cases. Polygamy is a great social curse. In many cases the more vigorous women and girls are taken into the harems of the chiefs and headmen, to the number of hundreds. As a result, the common men must select the less perfect, less vigorous women for their wives. Degeneracy of stock is the inevitable result.

Heathenism is intrenched in this lust of the flesh. Christianity, with its divine theory of home life, will make slow progress against it. But no compromise should be made; for it is an abnormal condition, and must yield to the onward sweep of human progress.

4. **War** is one of the great evils in the Dark Continent. Its petty chiefs rule over small bands or tribes. The ambition or anger of the former, or the weakness of the latter, occasions continual strife. The protectorate of foreign powers has done much to remove this evil by prohibiting the importation of arms and by police regulations adopted. It was necessary to save Africa from herself. Human life here has been very cheap for ages past. Self-restraint and a higher conception of the worth of a human being are necessary to remove this curse.

5. **Rum** in this hot climate and among this impulsive people is a curse too great to be fully understood. It is a greater curse here than in any other place. Stanley and others ascribe to this

CHIEF SOURRIE KESSEBE'S HOUSEHOLD.

cause much of the fatality to Europeans occurring here, and its deadly effect upon the African is even greater. Joseph Thompson said ten years ago: "In these facts lies the secret of the astonishingly small progress our west coast settlements have made." Bishop Ingham, formerly of Sierra Leone, says: "But for the rum and gin and gunpowder, which tend to the gendering of a worse bondage than of yore, we would bid emphatically Godspeed to the trade that has displaced the traffic in flesh and blood. If only these colonies *could* become strong enough in public opinion to protect themselves against the drink-traffic; if only a few more substantial African merchants *can* see their way to refuse to import spirits into their country; if only the government will become fully alive to the importance of saving the native tribes from enfeeblement in this respect, it is not even too late to erect a barrier against these noxious liquors." It is gratifying to know that efforts are being made to save Africa from this, one of her greatest, if not the greatest of her foes.

At the Brussels Conference of 1890-91 an international agreement was reached and an area from the twentieth degree north to the twenty-second degree south of the equator and extending across the continent was defined from which liquors are to be excluded. When this is thoroughly enforced, as it is now in some places, it will do more for Africa than all other good offices European nations have yet effected. It surely is a burning shame that Christian nations have so long held out with the right hand a rum bottle, while they have with the left hand offered the Bible to poor Africa.

6. **Slavery** Livingstone called "the open sore of Africa." Drummond called it "the heart-disease of Africa." So truly has it depleted her vitality. It is not the domestic slavery, which exists everywhere, but the traffic in slaves that makes this curse. Thanks to a good providence it has ceased on the Atlantic Coast by Christian nations quitting and forbidding the evil business. But the Mohammedan Arabs still inflict the curse upon a helpless people. Says Drummond: "Sometimes the Arab traders will actually settle for a year or two in the heart of some quiet community in the remote interior. They pretend perfect friendship; they molest no one; they barter honestly. They plant the seeds of their favorite vegetables and fruits,—the Arab always carries seeds with him,— as if they meant to stay forever. Meantime they buy ivory, tusk after tusk, until great piles of it are buried beneath their huts and all their barter goods are gone. Then one day suddenly the inevitable quarrel is picked. Then follows a wholesale massacre. Enough only are spared from the slaughter to carry the ivory to the coast; the grass huts of the villages are set on fire; the Arabs strike camp, and the slave-march, worse than death, begins."

The last act in the drama, the slave-march, is the aspect of slavery which in the past has chiefly aroused the passion and the sympathy of the outside world; but the greater evil is the demoralization and disintegration of communities by which it is necessarily preceded.

It is essential to the traffic that the region drained by the slaver should be kept in a perfect perpetual political ferment, that, in order to prevent combination, chief should be pitted against chief, and that the moment any tribe threatens to assume a dominating strength it should either be broken up by the instigation of rebellion among its dependencies or made a tool of at their expense. The interrelation of tribe with tribe is so intricate that it is impossible to exaggerate the effect of disturbing the equilibrium of even a single center. But, like a river, a slave caravan has to be fed by innumerable tributaries all along its course, at first in order to gather a sufficient volume of human bodies for the start, and afterwards to replace the frightful loss from desertion, disablement, and death.

Livingstone says: "It was wearisome to see skulls and bones scattered about everywhere; one would fain not notice them, but they are so striking as one trudges along the sultry path that it cannot be avoided."

Another says that you cannot miss the slaves' path; it is marked by human bones.

The great slave markets are now in Cairo, Mecca, and in other parts of the Turkish Empire. To supply these markets the Sudan furnishes fifty thousand, the Nile Valley sixty thousand, and east Africa at least forty thousand victims yearly. By conquest, by commerce, but, most of all, by the work and influence of Christian missions, this great crime against humanity must be brought to an end.

Mission Work in Africa is shown by the following tables taken from Thornton's book, his estimate of population being lower than that usually given:

Continental Divisions.	Area in Square Miles.	Population.	Protestant Missionaries.	
			European.	American.
Northern Africa (including the Sahara).........	3,989,630	27,315,000	161	49
The Great Sudan..........	2,127,180	55,920,000	229	25
Central Africa............	3,877,267	39,975,000	340	170
Southern Africa (including British Central Africa).....................	1,473,710	7,294,000	456	9
Totals...............	11,467,787	130,504,000	1,186	253

"Further: Northern Africa has one Protestant missionary to 125,000 Mohammedans. The Sahara has one Protestant missionary to 2,500,000 Mohammedans. The Sudan states have one Protestant missionary to 45,000,000 Mohammedans and pagans. West Africa has about one Protestant missionary to 30,000 pagans. Central Africa has one Protestant missionary to 80,000 pagans. Southern Africa has one Protestant missionary to 14,000 pagans. These missionaries come from forty Protestant missionary societies."

The Bible or parts of the Bible, is now translated into sixty languages and dialects of Africa.

CHAPTER II.

1. SIERRA LEONE IN GENERAL.

"**Sierra Leone** is a British crown colony on the west coast of Africa, lying between the seventh degree and the tenth degree north latitude, and from the tenth degree of west longitude to the coast. The words 'Sierra Leone' signify 'lion hill,' so called from the fancied resemblance of the peninsula to a lion. The peninsula is a high and rocky headland, thirty miles long by sea, and extending twenty miles up the Sierra Leone River, and skirted by alluvial lowlands that rise gradually and merge into the hills of the interior. The mountains of Sierra Leone are visible a long distance at sea. The green hills, covered with tropical vegetation, and dotted here and there with pretty villages and cultivated fields, are a beautiful and welcome sight to one accustomed to northern latitudes. The colony has a coast line of one hundred and eighty miles, and an estimated hinterland, or breadth, called a protectorate, of two hundred and fifty miles. It is about equal in area to the State of Ohio.

"**Freetown,** the capital, is a heavily fortified seaport town of forty thousand inhabitants, closely nestled against the hills at the mouth of the Sierra Leone River. It is an important naval and coaling station, and port of entry for the Sudan region, and is said to have the best harbor on the west coast of Africa. The town has broad streets, usually covered with grass, except a narrow path in the center, and is well lighted and watered, and can be well drained. The buildings are mostly detached cottages of wood, mud, or stone, or stone below and wood above, with iron or slate roofs.

"The Peninsula of Sierra Leone was ceded to Great Britain in 1787 by the native chiefs, as refuge for freed negroes from England and Nova Scotia, and those taken from slavers on the high seas. The colony has been enlarged to its present proportion by subsequent treaties with the chiefs of neighboring tribes. The more important of these tribes are the Susu, Gallinas, Temni, Mendi, and Sherbro. Constant and barbarous warfare existed all along this coast previous to the English occupation. To these tribes the English now give protection in times of war, in return for which these tribes are required to keep open roads and pay a small tax. Three English commissioners, assisted by five hundred native police, with white officers, exercise authority and guarantee peace. In local and distinctly tribal matters the authority of the native chief is seldom molested. The native system of government is very much like a patriarchal despotism, and domestic slavery is common. Beside the chiefs, are the head, or principal men, who consult and advise in all important matters. The general government of the colony is administered by a legislative and executive council, consisting of a governor, who is assisted by the various heads of departments, or colonial officers, and three citizens. The governor is appointed by the Queen's secretary of colonies, the others on the governor's approval.

"**The Manner of Life** in Freetown is prevailingly eastern. Each follows his inclination, careless of his fellow's wants. To all appearances, one steps into a bygone age when he lands upon these shores. English manners and customs have been adopted by a few. The descendants of the original colonists are called Sierra Leoneans, and form one-half the population. These are the traders, artisans, and professional men, and are altogether a bright, shrewd, and clever people. Freetown is one of the most cosmopolitan places on earth. No less than sixty distinct languages are spoken, while there are representatives of nearly a hundred. These come from all parts of the Sudan and central Africa. Many are brought down as slaves by caravan merchants, and for various reasons left here.

"It is a strange sight to see the mingling of the nations. There is every shade of complexion that black and white and brown will make. There is every variety of stature, feature, costume, and head-dress. Here is the tall 'Foulah,' his hair and scanty beard done up in little knotted pigtails; there the bold-featured, tattooed 'Krooman.' Here is the self-important Sierra Leonean, the savage Mandingo, and the shrewd Mohammedan priest; there, in little groups, the jabbering tradeswomen. All are straight and well-formed, from bearing burdens on their heads, and dressed in every color of the rainbow. There is an air of business about this city rarely seen in tropical countries; yet, even here, indolence is the preferable rule, and garrulity and demonstration a substitute for business.

"**The Carrying Trade** of the colony, on sea, is

by means of small sail-craft; on land, on the heads of natives. No beasts of burden or mechanical contrivances for lessening human labor are known among the black population. These small boats enter the many small rivers, and barter iron pots, knives, beads, tobacco, cheap cottons, etc., for rice, cola-nuts, rubber, and palm kernels. Other boats bring fish, fruits, and vegetables to the wharves, where tradeswomen and children buy, fill their calabashes, and go from house to house to sell. The mountains furnish many varieties of fruits and vegetables, which are disposed of in the same manner. Among fruits are the orange, banana, pineapple, sour-sop, sweet-sop, tamarind, papaw, mango, apple (not American), kushew, guava, plum, breadfruit, and pear (alligator). The principal vegetables are cassava, coca, potatoes (sweet), okra, cabbage, cucumbers, onions, lettuce, beans, garden eggs, tomatoes, and peppers.

"Caravans from beyond the Kong Mountains bring gold, ivory, ostrich feathers, gums, dyes, hides, and curios. Rice is the staple food of the whole people.

"Animals. As horses will not live on the coast, all travel is done on foot, or in the hammock, which is borne on the heads of four natives. There are only twenty miles of railroad in the colony. Narrow and exceedingly tortuous foot-paths are the only highways, and dugout canoes and foot-logs the only substitute for bridges. Transportation is costly, although labor can be had for twenty cents a day.

"The domestic animals are cattle, pigs, sheep, and goats, and are used only for food. Horses, asses, camels, elephants, and dromedaries are said to be plentiful away from the coast (far inland). The wild animals that can be said to be within the confines of the colony are the elephant, leopard, fox, wild hog, wild ox, several species of small deer, and several species of monkeys. Creeping things are abundant. Among the larger reptiles are the python, viper, the deadly cerastes, crocodile, iguana, and many aquatic species. The smaller ones include lizards, chameleons, centipedes, multipedes, and scorpions. The adaptability of reptiles to the color of their surroundings reaches its perfection here. Insects are not numerous, and, with the exception of the ant, not troublesome to human existence. The ant is pre-eminently master of Africa. More than a score of species occur, both diurnal and nocturnal, and their ravages are constantly seen.

"The feathered kingdom is represented by many aquatic and terrestrial species. Of the former are the pelican, ibis, heron, flamingo, crane, fish-eagle, duck, gull, and egret. Of the latter are the eagle, hawk, osprey, hornbill, crow, parrot, vulture, cow-bird, oriole, snipe, and pheasant. Among fish, we have the shark, porpoise, conter, redfish, mackerel, tenney, and the tropical herring, or 'bunger.' Animal life is not as abundant here as might be expected for the tropics. Forest fires are frequent during the dry season, and this is, doubtless, the reason for its scarcity.

"**The Flora** of Sierra Leone is varied, dense, and picturesque, but not beautiful. The ancient forests have been removed, and their giant and luxuriant vegetation replaced by a dense undergrowth of shrub. Where the devastations of man stop the truly tropical forest begins. Ancient and lordly trees interlock their branches hundreds of feet above, and all but conceal the sun. Vines, like great hawsers, wind among the branches, or, covered with foliage, drop in pendent festoons. Beasts of prey and huge reptiles lurk in the dense undergrowth, while troops of monkeys and beautifully plumaged birds inhabit the branches above.

"The forest wealth of the coast region of Sierra Leone is practically gone. Gum arabic, gum copal, indigo, cola-nuts, palm-oil, and rubber are obtained in considerable quantities. Some ivory is also obtained. The more important dye-woods and cabinet materials have largely disappeared. Mahogany, rosewood, and camwood are found in small quantities. Flowers are not beautiful or abundant. They blossom throughout the year, and are never appreciated, much less cultivated. The process of the terminal leaf developing into a blossom is seen here in its perfection. One species of rose changes from white in the morning to red in the evening. Every variety of leaf, petal, ovary, and arrangement of flowers is seen here.

"No precious metals have yet been found within the confines of the colony. There is a free distribution of iron and plumbago, but no deposits. The soil is red laterite, with a subsoil of gneiss.

"**The Protectorate of Sierra Leone** has an estimated population of 400,000, of whom 220 are Europeans, the others are natives. Of these, 41,000 are Christians, most of whom live in the peninsula of Sierra Leone, and are divided as follows: Episcopalians, 21,000; Methodists, of different bodies, 13,200; United Brethren in Christ, 6,000; Romanists, 570; Baptists, 190; Presbyterians, 384. There are about 20,000 Mohammedans, and the rest are pagans.

"The Educational Institutions are: Fourah Bay College, Anna Walsh School for Girls, the Technical School, and the Grammar and High Schools at Freetown; Rufus Clark and Wife Training School at Shaingay; High School at Rotufunk, and High School at Bonthe; the beginning of the technical schools at both Rotufunk and Shaingay, and the primary schools connected with every church and mission. Comparatively few of the youth are in the schools, but enough have been trained to show the possibilities and advantages of both technical and scholastic education for these children of nature.

"Sierra Leone is not destined to become great in agricultural or material prosperity, but Freetown is the gateway to west Africa, and what the opening up of the interior means to Great Britain and to commerce it means also to the kingdom of God and the spiritual welfare of her untutored millions."—*Fred. S. Minshall.*

2. Sierra Leone Tribes.

As our African missions are all within the British protectorate and Colony of Sierra Leone, it is desirable to describe it more fully, and to present most completely the parts of it in which we are most interested.

Sierra Leone Colony is but a small part of the Sierra Leone territory. It lies in north latitude eight degrees twenty minutes, and west longitude thirteen degrees twelve minutes. It is a peninsula twenty-six miles long, and of an average width of twelve miles. The Sierra Leone Mountains extend from northwest to southeast through its entire length, and rise in different peaks to two thousand and three thousand feet above the sea. These mountains constitute the larger part of the peninsula, and are covered by forest, except where cleared away by man.

Nestled in the little valleys on all sides are beautiful villages, each with its church and parish school. The gardens, hardly large enough to be called farms, produce vegetables and fruits in abundance.

Freetown has many public buildings of note, as St. George's Cathedral of the English Church, the Bishop's Court, and many other less noted churches; Fourah Bay College, a female college; the Wesleyan High School, a technical school; Wilberforce Hall, government buildings, and stores. Among the latter is the well-furnished store of Yates and Porterfield, of New York, who have shown our missions many favors, and whose energetic and courteous manager, Mr. Smart, until May, 1898, the American consul, is a devoted friend of our missionaries.

The governor's residence is here. The present incumbent is Colonel Frederick Cardew, C. M. G. He is a man of about sixty years, of iron frame and dignified bearing, with a face indicating courage, wisdom, practical tact, and generous sympathies; and to these he adds the other qualities of a courteous Christian gentleman. Not only from the statesman's policy, but from noble instincts, he

gives the full weight of his influence to the efforts of Christian missions among the natives. It is his custom to visit our missions and contribute to their support, as well as to invite our missionaries to visit him in his home and to dine with him. In company with other missionaries, we met at the governor's table the newly appointed bishop of Sierra Leone, the Rev. J. Taylor Smith, a man of noble Christian spirit, of wide culture, and of large experience in African mission work. Here, at the suggestion of our superintendent, Rev. J. R. King, and with the hearty approval of Bishop Smith, we planned a conference of all the missionaries in this region, which was held on February 1, 1897. About one dozen representatives of six different missionary societies were present, and an organization was effected. From such co-operation and mutual helpfulness much good will come. I met the other chief officers of this colony, and the commissioners and the police captains of the "Hinterland," all of whom extended the most courteous treatment and every assistance possible.

Leaving Freetown, off to the southwest a half-mile is a government botanical garden and farm, where experiments are being made and plants collected. Taking the fine military road east, we ascend the mountain, first passing the military barracks, where a regiment of soldiers is quartered; then on higher, we come to a village. The people come out of their little cottages to salute with a "How do, sa?" After due response, they reply, "Thank ee, sa; good day, sa." And the little children are met along the street, begging for a penny. This begging business is a common feature among the natives almost everywhere you meet them. But it is no greater humbug here than the "tips" demanded everywhere in Europe.

This Military Road is as fine as any wagon road with us, and can be followed up to a path within three hundred yards of the English Church's sanitarium, on the side of Mount Leicester. Near this is the Catholic sanitarium, and a little over one hundred yards above the Catholic is our own sanitarium. It is owned jointly by our two mission boards. The corner-stones of the buildings were laid November 4, 1896, in the presence of a distinguished body of Americans, Englishmen, and natives. The building was christened "Bethany Cottage." The Americans and English then proceeded to the English sanitarium for lunch, and in the evening the Americans were invited to dine with Mr. Guyer and Mr. and Mrs. Smart, of the firm of Yates & Porterfield, in honor of the election of President McKinley, which occurred the day before.

But to return to Bethany Cottage—it is located on a piece of ground once cleared of brush and the rocks removed for a British barracks. It is sixteen hundred feet above the sea, and about four miles from the wharf. It is of easy access by hammock or on foot. The building is of stone, with an iron roof, and large enough for its purpose. At this altitude the air is pure, and the nights are delightfully cool. The vision spread out before the observer is one of the most beautiful to be found anywhere. To the east, Mount Leicester rises four hundred feet higher; to the west, lies the ocean, stretching to the most distant verge of vision, at certain hours shimmering in the sunshine like a sea of gold, flecked with steamers and smaller boats; to the north, across Bullòm shore, on up the coast, the vision extends to a distant range of hazy mountains; then, lying between the ocean and your feet, is the lively mountain side, with its ever dark green robe, variegated with villages, cottages, and gardens— below these, the city of Freetown embowered in its feathery palms and other tropical trees and plants. We could not find a more lovely spot in west Africa where our weary missionaries may come and rest awhile with Him who loved to visit that other Bethany cottage in the olden time.

The two mission boards have also a dwelling-house rented in Freetown. As this is the place of landing and departure for our missionaries, and the port of entry for our supplies, and the most important port for the Sudan country, it seems desirable that we should own a home down in the city and a church for the success of our work inland, as well as to aid in evangelizing this center whose heathen population grows more rapidly than its civilized citizens.

Leaving Sierra Leone Colony, let us take a survey of the other parts included in the British protectorate of this region, giving most space to the tribes among which our missions operate.

The Sherbros, Bulloms, and Lokkohs seem to be of the same stock and to have formerly been one tribe. Their language and customs are similar. They occupy the coast region from the Great Skarcies River north of Sierra Leone, almost of the Sulima River in the south, nearly down to Liberia (except the peninsula of Sierra Leone itself).

The Susus occupy the coast north of the Great Skarcies River, and extend far into Senegambia. They are a powerful tribe, of a tawny color, and of Foulah origin.

The Limbas are directly east of the Susus. They are the descendants of slaves formerly belonging to the Susus and Mandingoes. They are very numerous, but not as enterprising as either of their former masters.

The Kurankoes, or Mandingoes, occupy the country east of the Limbas, and extend far away into the French territory. They were one of the most powerful tribes along the valley of the Gambia when conquered by the Portuguese in 1420. "Some of that nation settled here and intermixed with the natives, so that the Mandingoes consider themselves almost white, though ever so black." This tribe is one of the most vigorous of the natives. The Susus, the Limbas, and the Mandingoes occupy the whole of the north part of the Sierra Leone protectorate. Their territory has been but little visited by Europeans, and hence not much is known of the land or the people. There are several hundred thousand souls in these tribes, and hardly a Christian missionary among them, but the Mohammedans are pushing into this region.

The Temni country lies east and northeast of the peninsula of Sierra Leone, on both sides of the Rokel River, extending across the protectorate, and is eighty miles wide from north to south. While the eastern part of their country has not yet been explored, the tribe has been well known for over one hundred years. It was from one of their chiefs that the British obtained the peninsula in

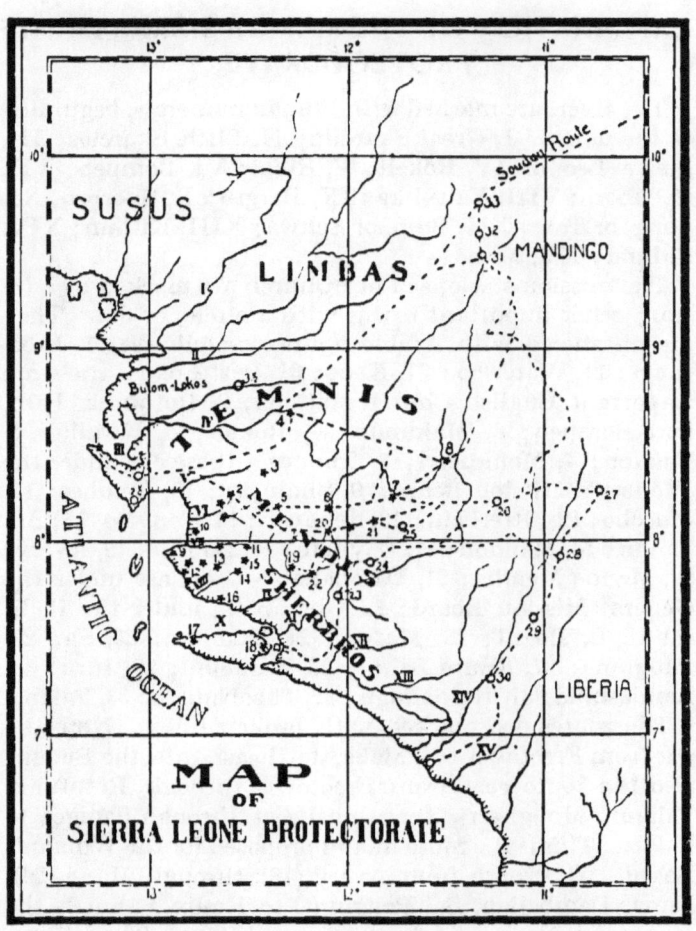

EXPLANATION OF THE MAP OF SIERRA LEONE PROTECTORATE.

The rivers are marked with Roman numerals, beginning at the north. I, Great Skarcies; II, Little Skarcies; III, Sierra Leone; IV, Rokell; V, Ribbi; VI, Bompeh; VII, Cockboro; VIII, Yaltukka; IX, Bargru; X, Sherbro; XI, Jong, or Taia; XII, Bum, or Schwa; XIII, Kittam; XIV, Sulima; XV, Mano.

The mission stations of our Church are marked by a (*) star; other important towns with a circle, or dot. They are numbered with Arabic figures, as follows: 1, Freetown; 1½, Waterloo; 2½, Kent; 3½, Port Loko — these are important English Church stations; 2, Rotufunk, Palli, and Bompeh; 3, Makundo; 4, Rokon; 5, Kwallu; 6, Taiama; 7, Mongherri; 8, Tungea — these are under the Woman's Mission Board; 9, Shaingay; 10, Rembee; 11, Mocobo; 12, Otterbein; 13, Jehovah; 14, Tongolo, 15; Ma Sandu; 16, Maudoh; 17, Daymah; 18, Bouthe; 19, Avery; 20, Mano (Mendi); 21, Damballah — these are under the General Mission Board; 22, Gbambiah, under the Radical U. B. Board; 23, Mafwa; 24, Tikonko; 25, Sa; 26, Panguma; 27, Kaure Lahm; 28, Yandahu; 29, Juru; 30, Bandasuma; 31, Koinadugu; 32, Tobabadugu; 33, Falaba.

The routes are marked with broken lines. Note the one from Freetown to Falaba, northeast, into the Sudan; also the route east from Freetown through Rotufunk, Taiami, Mongherri, then northeast through Tungea to Falaba. This is the route inland proposed for the Woman's Board. The route from Avery (19), through Mano (20), Jama, Damballah, Sa, Panguma, to Kaure Lahm is the route inland proposed for the General Board. The railway is now completed from Freetown to Waterloo, and it is proposed to run it on through Rotufunk, Taiama, Mongherri, and Panguma, to the east limit of the Protectorate.

1787. Their present numbers are estimated at over one hundred thousand. They are fond of war, are of superior mental and physical strength, and appear anxious to have their children educated in the mission schools, often sending them a long distance for this purpose. Their language has been reduced to writing, and part of the Bible published in it, by Rev. J. A. Alley, an English missionary, stationed at Port Loko. Also, the Rev. C. F. Schlenker, a German, but employed by an English missionary society, has published a work entitled, "Temni Traditions and Vocabulary."

The Mendi people live south of the Temnis, and from the Sherbros south and east to Liberia. The great road from Freetown east to Panguma is near the north boundary of the Mendi country, the Temnis overlapping this road in some places. In a general way, this road may be regarded as the boundary between these two tribes. The population of this region is but little less than that of the Temni country. The two tribes do not differ much in general traits of character. The Mendi language also has been reduced to a written form by a missionary, and some books have been printed in it.

The Sherbro, Mendi, and Temni are the tribes among which our missions are operating. They belong to the great negro, or Sudanese, stock. It will not be surprising if some time we shall discover a common home in central Africa from which these tribes migrated westward. The Sherbros occupy the most unhealthful region along the coast, where the rivers are sluggish, swamps abound, and malarial poison fills the air. The vigorous Mendis and Temnis are crowding the Sherbros down to the coast, and it is highly probable that the latter tribe will be absorbed in less than one hundred years. It is also highly probable that as war and slave-trading are abolished by European authority, the tribes in the different protectorates will mingle together more than in the past, though much mixing now occurs, in spite of tribal hatred. It is easy for a whole town to move to another location in a single dry season. Their huts are so easily built that a week or two of labor provides a new domicile. The family goods can easily be carried away, as the chiefs hold all the land. Hence motives which bind white men to their homes have little or no influence here. This migrating tendency is illustrated by a little incident of personal experience. When the writer was leaving Dayton, Ohio, for Africa, two years ago, he was asked to visit Mambo, where the Sunday school of Summit Street Church, of Dayton, was supporting a school. In due time Mambo was visited. It is an isolated place, up the Cockboro River, and had not been visited by a white man for two years. The mission-house, which had been built of native materials, was a heap of clay, overgrown with weeds high as one's head; the town was deserted, except about three houses occupied by Sierra Leonean traders; the other buildings were in ruins, and, as if in despair, a huge cotton-tree ten feet in diameter, an object of native superstitious reverence, had fallen prone across the landing.

This habit of moving explains the removal of some mission-posts, and enforces the wisdom of erecting only clay houses at the smaller towns; for these the natives are usually ready to build, if the missionary will provide a pastor and teacher.

The Kroomen should be mentioned before leaving this subject. Their home is on the coast, several hundred miles further south, but they have a large colony on the south side of Freetown. They are the sailors of the west coast. Strong and vigorous, they are very handy in loading and unloading ships, and are sought for such service by the European vessels. They are also in demand as boatmen, laborers, servants, and cooks. "Their distinguishing mark is a black line running from the forehead down the face, along the ridge of the nose, and continuing through the upper and lower lips and chin, and the barb of an arrow represented on each side of the temple. The body is also generally tattooed in a fanciful manner."

3. NATIVE SOCIETY, LANGUAGE, CUSTOMS, ETC.

Society includes the two factors—persons and environment.

1. The environment includes: (1) Configuration of surface. Along the coast, except the mountains in the peninsula, the surface is flat, the numerous rivers move sluggishly, and swamps are common. Forty to fifty miles inland the surface rises, and still farther inland, hills, peaks, and considerable mountains in isolated or irregular groups, are found. The rivers move more swiftly, and numerous rapids occur. (2) The climate means the heat and cold, the moisture and drouth, the light and darkness of any given region. Here the temperature averages about ninety-five degrees at noonday, in the shade, and about sixty-five de-

grees at midnight, through the year, except in January and February, when a cool wind from the continent blows, called the harmattan. During this period the thermometer, at noon, frequently marks but seventy-five degrees, the air is filled with a fine dust through which, in the morning and evening, the sun looks red—a perfect American Indian summer. No frost ever visits this region, but the early mornings and nights are usually cool and pleasant. The natives, who are fond of warmth, usually have fire in their huts every night throughout the year. It is not the excessive heat, but the continuous heat that is oppressive to the white man. The moisture is excessive and drouth is unknown. The rain falls for six months, from May till October, with another month to begin on, and one to taper off. There are heavy dews the balance of the year, and enough moisture. At Freetown the rainfall is from 125 to 175 inches each year, and it probably averages the latter figures every year all over this region. The light and darkness are equally divided, and the native spends more time in sleep than is common in America. (3) The fauna and flora are described elsewhere. Their utilization by the natives is barely sufficient to maintain life on a low plane. As a rule, the necessaries of life are easily obtained, and no sufficient motive exists to induce the native to struggle for more. The climate is against him; the malarial poison in the air affects the black man as well as the white, though it is more injurious to the latter, and further, public opinion does not favor the accumulation of riches. On the coast this sentiment has been modified by contact with Europeans; but inland if one family should raise more rice than it could consume, with no immediate market, the neighbors would probably feel it their right or duty to go in and help to consume the surplus.

2. The stock is the negro, having various local names and customs; in the lowlands and swamps he has degenerated under the blighting effects of his environment, but in the higher country inland, he has developed more vigor and ability, yet remains substantially the same, in his native condition, everywhere. The one word that most fully expresses his nature in heathenism is, with few exceptions, childhood. He is as affectionate, trustful, hopeful, excitable, impulsive, vivacious, and thoughtless—lives in his senses and emotions—as a child.

Languages. In the colony the English language predominates. But with the uneducated part of the natives it is a kind of Pidgin-English, which is as difficult for the uninitiated to speak or understand as any other foreign tongue. As an illustration: I had preached twice at Bonthe before the conference sermon. The evening before this event, one of the teachers, Thomas Davis, announced to the natives that I would preach on the morrow, and that Rev. F. S. Minshall would be ordained, and this is the way he did it: "Dat big man wot com out fr' 'meric go preach marin. Wot he preach 'fore no preach 'tall, he so pass it. An' nah man wot come wi' 'im he go turn into godman, gud fashion. Come one time, w'en bell sound,"—this uttered in a tone and rapidity equal to a Frenchman's. This jargon, of which the above is a better sample than usual, is the trade English up and down the coast. The following is a native letter, furnished by Miss Kingsley:

"To Daddy nah Tampin office. Ha Daddy, do, yah, nah beg you tell dem people for me; make dem Sally-own pussin know. Do yah. Berrah well.

"Ah lib nah Pademba Road—one bwoy lib dah oberside lakah dem two Docter lib overside you Tampin office. Berrah well.

"Dah bwoy head big too much—he say nah Militie Ban—he got one long long ting so so brass, someting lib dah go flip-flap, dem call am key. Berrah well. Had! Dah bwoy kin blow! She ah! nah marin, oh! nah sun time, oh! nah evenin' oh! nah middle night, oh!—all same—no make pussin sleep. Not ebry bit dat, more lib da! One Bony bwoy lib oberside nah he like blow bugle. When dem two woh-woh bwoy blow dem ting de nize too much, too much.

"When white man blow dat ting and pussin sleep he kin tap wah make dem bwoy carn do so? Dem bwoy kin blow ebry day, eben Sunday dem kin blow. When ah yerry dem blow Sunday ah wish dah bugle kin go down no dem troat or dem kin blow them hed-bone inside.

"Do nah beg you yah tell all dem people 'bout dah ting wah dem two bwoy dah blow. Till am Amtruny Boboh had febah bad. Till am tilly carn sleep nah night. Dah nize go kill me two pickin, oh!

"Plabba done, Good by Daddy.
"Crashey Jame."

By knowing that the writer is complaining of two boys who are annoying her and her children almost to death by practicing on a bugle and trombone, and then by reading the letter aloud, its meaning may be understood.

Of course good English is taught in the schools, but it is difficult to convince the native or the average Sierra Leonean, that their style of English is not superior. In both the Mendi and the Sherbro countries is found, in every town, some one who can talk a little English. This is due to the two facts, that nearly every man in the protectorate has at some time visited Freetown (and many of them visit it yearly, to see and to hear, and to exchange the load of rice carried on his head and back, or the items carried in his boat) and that the missionary, or the trader, or the policeman has been everywhere.

The native languages are said to be picturesque in description, vigorous in construction, and melodious in sound. In all our congregations, in preaching, the American missionaries have to use interpreters. This is often very unsatisfactory when the regular interpreter is absent. Bishop Flickinger was once preaching on the parable, "I am the vine, and ye are the branches," when the whole effect of the sermon was lost by the interpreter rendering the text, "I am the rope, ye are the threads." I was once preaching at Deymah, with John Remmie for interpreter. As he had been the cook at Shaingay mission for twenty years it was thought he understood well both Sherbro and English. I was told, afterward, by one of the natives, that in the middle of the discourse, when I thought that John was translating what I had said, he told the congregation, "I hope you understand what the Bishop said, I do not." At another time a missionary was up country and asked a trader whom he met there, and who professed to be a Christian, to interpret for him. The missionary lost some confidence in traders, when a few weeks later he returned to this place, and was informed by a native that the trader had not rendered the sermon at all, but had taken the occasion to advertise his own business, and to give the prices he was paying for palm, and cola-nuts.

It is much to be regretted that our missionaries, in the beginning of our African work, were not instructed to learn the language of the people among whom they labored. And it is gratifying to know that Miss Cronise, Miss Eaton, and Mrs. McGrew, at Rotufunk, and Mrs. Howard, at Shaingay, and Mrs. King, at Bonthe, have made, recently, a fair beginning in the study of the Temni, Mendi, and Sherbro languages. From the success of these ladies in other lines of work, and from their recognized ability and zeal, we may expect much to result from their linguistic labors.

The Native Customs of the three tribes of which I am speaking do not differ much, except as one has been influenced by contact with foreign ideas more than the others.

(1) **Domestic** customs are such as relate to family life. Polygamy is the prevailing marriage state of the negro. No such thing as courtship is known, but the man, if a chief, adds whom he pleases to his harem, as parents are glad to have their daughters in such households. Some chiefs, (as Nygwa, at Panguma,) are said to rival Solomon in the number of their wives. The ordinary

man must deal with the parents and pay about fifteen dollars apiece for his wives. Polygamy is one of the chief hindrances to the spread of Christianity, and one of the chief causes of the conquests of Mohammedanism among the negroes. But it is intrenched in three great facts difficult for us to meet: The first is the "impossibility for one African woman to do the work of the house, prepare the food, fetch the water, cultivate the farm, and look after the children attributive to one man. She might do it if she could do the work one white woman can do, but this she cannot do. This leads her not to care a fig how many women have her man's attention so long as he gives her as much cloth and beads as any of the others receive. She reasons, the more women the less work, and is satisfied." The second fact is the one well known to ethnologists, that the negro, when he knows that his wife is to give birth to a child, lives separate from her till after that child is weaned; and he thinks he must have another wife to live with during this interval. The third fact is, that public opinion favors the plurality of wives by making a man's standing depend, to some extent, on it.

The clothing of the male youth and adults is a breech-cloth or a "country cloth," similar to an Indian's blanket; for the younger females it is sometimes as meager as a string of beads around the loins, from which hangs, in front, an apron four by six inches; others, and especially the married women, wear a country cloth, covering from the waist to the knees. The hot climate and poverty account for the limited clothing, and however fastidious the taste of the missionaries, best results will be reached by not requiring the natives to wear more than a loose, flowing gown at present. Contact with foreigners will finally change, somewhat, native tastes and customs of dress. Their country cloth is made from heavy, strong cotton thread, spun by hand aided by a stick a foot long. The weaving is equally primitive. The cloth is very durable, and usually striped blue and white, or black and white. They also weave mats from grasses, barks, and leaves.

The children go almost, if not entirely, naked till ten or twelve years old. Their chief clothing is a "little grease on their heads and a few flies on their backs." Either their food is so innutritious, or their appetites are so ravenous, they eat so much, that, after a meal, their abdomens are greatly distended. Circumcision is universally practiced, and if it is not performed in childhood the lad seems to feel ashamed of this fact till it is performed. The children aid the women in their work, and as long as the parents live the children feel under obligation to obey their wishes. They are very jealous of the honor of their fathers. One of the most frequent causes of palaver for the missionaries to settle among the black children is the charge made by one against another, "He cursed me daddy." Any word spoken against another's father is called a curse. Also for one boy to stick out his tongue at another boy is the same as uttering a curse. (The origin of this latter I could not learn, but learned that at Rotufunk it often caused a fight among the smaller boys.)

Among the Sherbros, the children, in all families, receive the same names, as follows: Boys—1,

Cho; 2, Thong; 3, Saw; 4, Barkey; 5, Reekeh; 6, Gbokah; girls—1, Boy; 2, Yamah; 3, Conah; 4, Marhen; 5, Chorcor; 6, Marner; 7, Yorkee. These names may all be given to the offspring of one woman; then they bear her name also, to distinguish them from the children of other mothers in the same family.

The houses are now rarely built isolated from each other; and until British protection was extended, they were always in towns, surrounded by a wall made of earth or wicker-work. The houses are made by setting in the ground poles eight or ten feet long, inclosing a round or square space of the desired size, say, fifteen feet in diameter. These poles stand near each other, and are woven together with vines and branches; then this wall receives on the outside a coat of mud four to six inches thick, and a similar one on the inside. The lower ends of the rafters are fastened with vines to the top of the walls, their upper ends coming together above, or resting on a cross-beam. The rafters are then covered with vines, or bamboo poles, as we place lath, and these are then covered with a special kind of grass, or, in its absence, with shingles made of palm leaves. If desired, the walls may receive a coat of whitewash, and sometimes a black band, two feet wide, extends around the bottom of the wall. This black coat is made of cow-dung, of which the earthen floor also receives a coat, in the belief that it keeps away vermin. A hole is left in the wall for a door, and another for a window; they are each closed by a grass mat hanging from the top of the opening. The bed is made of clay, and raised a few inches above the floor. The only covering is a thin grass mat. A few pegs in the wall, on which to hang things, and a simple stool make up the furniture of this average house. Just outside the house is a small kitchen, whose only furnishing is an iron pot in which to carry water and cook the food. The latter usually consists of rice, seasoned with fish, fowl, any kind of flesh, or palm-oil, and red pepper enough to make a white man cry over each bite he takes. It is a luxury, if there is a big wooden bowl in which to cool the food. It is then surrounded by the family, sitting on the ground, or standing, each of whom dips his hands into the food and carries it to his mouth. The cassava is eaten raw, or roasted in the hot ashes, or made into foo-foo, a most horrid food. The fruits are all eaten raw, except the plantain, which is best roasted. If any corn is raised, it is usually eaten parched.

Now one man has as many houses as he has wives, and they are most frequently in different towns; though, if he is a chief, he may have them all in the same town.

A collection of such houses, with a public hall, or barra, and the superior but similar houses of the chief, are crowded close together, without regard to order or streets, and more resemble a collection of haystacks and ricks, on one of our thriving farms, than anything else one can think of. These towns are nearly always near a pond or stream of water, as they dig no wells, except a hole in the bed of a stream, to accumulate the water flowing there. If the stream serves the purpose, the men have a bathing place on one side of the town, and the women have a similar place on the other side. They are very fond of a daily bath; but the women carry the big pot down to the river, and after the ablution of the whole body, they dip the water for cooking the food out of the same stream. The family washing occurs at the same place, and is done by wetting the clothes, and then beating them against a log.

Their houses are warmed by a fire built in the center of the floor, the smoke escaping at the roof. Their cutlass is not a good instrument for chopping. It quite resembles a corn-cutter. Hence, to save labor, they place one end of one stick against the end of another stick, and push them together as the fire consumes them. I saw such a fire in Chief Pa Sourri's house. In this case, one of the logs extended through the door into the yard. The land is owned by the chiefs. They must give permission before it can be farmed, built on, or a grave dug in it.

(2) **The Religious Customs** and theories of the negroes have been overlaid by Mohammedan and Christian ideas to such an extent that it is difficult to determine what is original and what is borrowed.

The majority of the natives believe in a supreme god, who is sometimes identified with the sun, the sky, or the ocean. To him the creation of the world is ascribed, and about him are grouped inferior gods, the forces or objects of nature personified, as lightning, thunder, the rainbow, lakes, rivers, springs, birds, serpents, animals, and the souls of the dead.

The spirits which animate the trees, the waters, the beasts, or the stones—in short, every object

which manifests a force or a power is conceived of
as separate from the plant, the animal, the stone,
or the river in which it is incarnated, and it can
also, like the souls of the dead, be constrained by
sacrifices, or can itself choose to inhabit any small
material object, which then becomes a fetish and
is worshiped because a god resides in it. The one
who owns one of these fetishes has at his control
the god who resides in it. Besides these individual
fetishes there are those belonging to families;
others, to towns; others, to tribes. They may cease
to be effective by the spirit dying, or by some
stronger inducement being offered the spirit to desert its former home and go to a more attractive
one. The negro is always in fear lest his tutelary
god forsake him and go to some enemy or rival.
When he is convinced that such a change has occurred he is ready to sell his fetish to some white
man as a curio; and then he hires a witch-doctor to
make him a stronger one. The infinite number of
spirits with which the world is peopled are good
and bad, malevolent and benevolent. The ill will
of the one kind can be propitiated, and the good
will of the other can be secured by the aid of the
sorcerers (witch-doctors) and by sacrifices. They
are not so much concerned about the supreme God,
the "one King," as they are anxious about the good
will of the nature spirits, and the spirits of dead
men, especially of dead sorcerers, chiefs, or great
warriors. The caves, the forests, especially the
great cotton-trees, the mountains, and the floods
are sacred to these spirits. The "devil house" at
the side of every town is the place where the guardian spirit of that town dwells and receives offer-

ings. They judge all these tutelary gods by their own natures, and they treat them accordingly. They believe these spirits can be controlled by offerings or by conjuring. Sometimes one sees a cotton string drawn across a highway or around a town, for which some sorcerer is well paid to keep away some evil spirit.

They universally believe in the survival of the soul after death. But the doctrine of a resurrection of the body is not known among them. The dead hold the same social position they held in this life; for example, a chief remains a chief, a slave remains a slave. Their worship is ritualistic in character, and consists of prayers and invocations, offerings, and sacrifices. They all wear fetishes, Mohammedan charms, or amulets of some kind—each particular kind for a particular purpose,—and they all believe in, and greatly dread fetish alligators and fetish leopards, that is, evil spirits having the body of these animals.

It may also be that their numerous dances have some religious significance. It is certain that no white man can admire them for gracefulness or beauty of movement. The mourning for the dead, a social custom practiced everywhere in this region, may have some religious purpose. At Mongherri I saw the women mourning for the deceased chief, and heard their doleful lamentations away into the night. They sat on the ground and swung their bodies back and forward, uttering a pitiful wail. It was said this would be kept up for one year, then each wife might select any son or brother of the late chief and live in his home; if any one of them made no choice, she might be selected by any relative of the deceased.

Belief in witchcraft or sorcery is universal, and is a source of much misery. It is highly probable that the secret of the professional witch-doctor is not in his supernatural power, but in his secret knowledge and use of poisons. The gall of the alligator and of the leopard, and caliboa beans are supposed to be the usual sources of the poison, to which we may add the vemon of snakes.

Even in Freetown, Bishop Ingham says: "Such mutual distrust still prevails among the people, that no one seems ever supposed to have died a natural death.

"It is hard to say that poisoning is actually attempted on any large scale. Certainly it is widely feared. Nothing goes to prove this so much as the fact that people do not eat in one another's houses, except at a large spread, when there is safety in numbers."

Witch-doctor and professional poisoner are synonymous terms, and the British are doing well in getting rid of them. I saw two being led away to death, and heard of others in prison, awaiting trial.

3. **The Native Legal Customs** are not uniform. The Porroh Society has long been the popular legislative body; other laws were made by local chiefs; still others by a number or all of the chiefs of a tribe; but the Porroh Society's laws were supreme. They have no jails or other places for confining prisoners.

Every death is apt to be attributed to witchcraft. Miss Kingsley thinks that the belief in witchcraft is the cause of more African deaths than anything else. "It has killed more than the slave trade. Its only rival is, perhaps, smallpox." Some one dies, "the witch-doctor is called in, and he proceeds to find out the guilty person. Then woe to the unpopular men, the weak women, and slaves, for on some of them will fall the accusation that means ordeal by poison or fire, followed, if these point to guilt, as from their nature they usually do, by a terrible death." Whether the method varies with the tribe or with the individual witch-doctor is not certain; probably with the latter. In some parts of west Africa the witch-doctor goes round a village ringing a small bell, which is to stop ringing outside the hut of the guilty. In other places the witch-doctor puts on and takes off the lid of a small box while he repeats the names of all the people of the village. When the lid refuses to come off at the name of a person, that person is doomed. Another witch-doctor rubs the palms of his hands against each other. When the palms refuse to meet at a name, and fly wildly apart, he has his man.

The accused person, if he denies his guilt and does not claim the ordeal, is tortured till he not only acknowledges his guilt, but names his accomplices in the murder, for witchcraft is murder in their eyes. That under these exciting conditions many a one confesses that he is guilty of witchcraft finds its parallel in the Salem witchcraft episode in our own country, and finds its explanation in the influence of current belief and hypnotic suggestion.

The ordeal in one place is to drink the cup of poison made from a decoction of the fresh bark of sasswood, a native tree. The only escape from its deadly effect is to privately dash (tip) the witch-doctor, so he will allow the drink to settle before administering it. If the man recovers he is declared innocent, but if he dies he is believed guilty. Another ordeal is the swallowing of three fish-hooks fastened together, so the points stand in different directions. They are swallowed down about four or five inches, then if they can be pulled out of the throat without catching, the party is declared innocent, but if they catch in his throat, he is punished for the crime. Still another ordeal of which I heard is to take a solemn oath that he is innocent of the accusation, with threatened death in the near future, by thunder and lightning, if guilty. The old witch-doctor having a monopoly of this last ordeal is so greatly feared that almost any other ordeal is preferred.

In other tribes the accused persons are given a trial before the chief and his headmen, who, acting as a jury, determine the guilt or innocence of the accused. In such trials any one may bear witness or make a plea. The trials are brief, and the penalty certain.

Among the Mendis the penalty for stealing was formerly the chopping off of the hand of the criminal. In a journey through this tribe, of twenty days' duration, and sleeping in the native huts without any locks on doors, not a pin was stolen from our party. In this same tribe the penalty for adultery was formerly the death of both parties.

The native chiefs formerly visited swift and severe penalties. The natives, with their strong impulses and weak wills, are no more prepared than children to enjoy the liberty of civilization. For this reason the time and space borderland between heathenism and civilization will always be in a worse moral condition than pure heathenism, —a sort of breaking up between winter and summer.

Throughout the protectorate the British have instituted a plan of law and order, administered by European commissioners and three kinds of courts of justice. The Court of the Native Chiefs follows native customs, with their former harshness removed, the death penalty being taken out of their hands. This court has jurisdiction of all minor offenses committed by natives. The Court of District Commissioner and Native Chiefs is presided over by the commissioner, who is assisted by two or more chiefs named by the governor, and has jurisdiction in all capital offenses arising among the natives. The Court of the District Commissioner is presided over by the commissioner, and has jurisdiction chiefly in matters relating to foreigners, to land, or to tribe differences.

4. MISCELLANEOUS MATTERS.

1. Secret Societies are numerous all over western Africa. The Porroh is the largest and is exclusively for men. Their lodges are near the towns in a dense woods, over which the society has full control. On the side next to the road a barricade of branches, and a mat hanging over an opening leading into the grove, and a few mystic symbols nearby, indicate the presence of the "devil bush," as it is called. None but the initiated or candidates are allowed to enter the lodge. An initiation takes place annually, during which the eligible boys and young men, after a training in the secret work of the society for several months, come out with much pride and pomp as Porroh men. I am told that they are trained in the native, civil, and parliamentary law. It seems to have been originally the popular lawmaking body of the land, with power even to limit the authority of the chiefs.

The chief man in a lodge is called the Porroh devil. He is masked, and blows a sort of trumpet which makes a loud and horrible sound. When the society marches, this trumpet is heard; then every man not a member of the society, if on the road, must turn his back to the advancing company and place his hands over his eyes, or suffer such penalty as they see fit to inflict. At the same time the women and children must retire to their houses and stand with faces in a corner and hands over their eyes, or suffer the consequences. The design is to prevent any one not a member looking upon the Porroh devil and his followers. This keeps the natives in doubt as to the origin of the fearful noise made and enables the society to terrorize the people.

The Bundoo Society is exclusively for women. Its lodges are similar to those of the former society, but are always in another grove, and in the depth of the forest. It is said that here the young girls are for months trained in the knowledge of a few simple medicines, undergo a sort of female circumcision, and are taught the mysteries of motherhood. The girls stay in the woods during this period. All that the public hears of them is an occasional weird chant coming from the distant lodge. Their initiation is supposed to fit them for marriage. It seems also to teach them some secret religious ceremonies and beliefs.

The head woman is held in high distinction, and during the annual lodge meeting she wears a black mask for her whole body and limbs, made of long fibers of bark, and wears a wooden mask covering her head and face. This face mask has Egyptian features.

The Wundi Society is for both sexes, and seems to be merely for social recreation. We met it frequently in the Mendi country. In towns where we lodged, on moonlit nights, they kept us awake by their dancing all night to a very monotonous tune, sung, beat on the drums, and aided by a bunch of dry switches held in either hand and clashed together.

The Leopard Society is a secret cannibal society, which existed in the Imperi country. The candidate for initiation furnished some one for the cannibalistic feast, and certain parts of the victim were then used for fetish purposes. Three men were hanged for cannibalism, in connection with this society in this region, in 1895. Rev. D. K. Wilberforce largely aided the British authorities in destroying this society throughout the protectorate.

The Alligator Society was another secret cannibal organization. There is a tradition that this society used a submarine boat and simulated an alligator in securing its victims. This society is now destroyed.

I heard of several other secret societies, such as the Yasi, the Humoi, the Ujai, and one among the Temnis, whose object is said to be to destroy all feeble or deformed children and incurably diseased persons. But these are so little known to me that I reserve them for future treatment, by some one more fully informed.

2. **The Money** of the natives was, until the British currency was introduced, cowrie shells, leaf tobacco, beads, and muslin and calico. These items, especially the beads and dry-goods, are still valuable for exchange to one going inland.

3. **Dancing** is a universal passion among the natives. In the societies, sometimes the men dance by themselves; in others, the women dance by themselves; while in others the sexes dance together. There are also dance girls, who seem to be slaves taken around the country to amuse the observers and secure a collection, or kept by chiefs to entertain their guests, as in the case of Madam Yoko, a noted female chief at Senahu. The dance girl is half nude, and has small bells around her ankles. Her dance is a shuffling movement, forward and backward, then a swift whirl clear around, and a sudden stamp with the right heel. At other times it is a continuous, rapid whirl around and around. Other athletic sports are cultivated by young men. On a sandy beach of the Schwa River, I saw men exercising. The prize-taker turned ten somersaults backwards, in succession. Many of them are very fleet on foot.

4. **Their Music** consists almost wholly in the time element, varied by low or loud noise. The drum is the chief native instrument, made of a piece of a hollow log with skin stretched over one end, the other end resting on the ground. Sometimes a section of a hollow log, like a barrel without heads, is used for a drum. I have also seen among them a sort of wooden piano, the keys made

of pieces of hard wood of different lengths, and played by striking on the keys with a hard stick, or hammer. But this seems to be of Mohammedan origin.

Contrary to expectation, they have very poor voices for singing. Professor Howard, at Shaingay, told me he could hardly find enough voices among one hundred and fifty students, to make a fair quartet. They all sing, of course, in their way. On the boat they frequently keep stroke to the music of their songs. These songs are generally made up as they go along, either some compliment to their chief guest, or some joke at his expense.

5. **Of Diseases,** Doctor Archer informed me that the most common is venereal disease, for which the natives have no adequate remedy. African fever is a form of malarial fever, and is more destructive to the whites than to the blacks. The latter use much red pepper in their food, and it seems to have a preventive effect in the case of the fever. They also have herbs from which they make a tea which breaks up the fever. The natives have no knowledge of surgery, and suffer much from this lack.

6. **Their Hospitality** is a noted trait. While at Rokon, the chief gave us lodging in his guest-chamber, a large circular room having seven good beds under canopies, ranged around the wall of the room. He also gave us rice, fruit, and a sheep. This was in the Temni country. The Mendis furnished us houses for lodging everywhere we went among them, and the chiefs nearly always made an address of welcome. At Dumballa they gave

us a sheep. In the Sherbro country we were among our missions, where, of course, the treatment was cordial. In the homes of such native pastors as Wiberforce, Taylor, Williams, Johnson, Morrison, Inskip, and Bickersteth, I ate with relish and slept in peace.

CHAPTER III.

OUR MISSION WORK IN SIERRA LEONE.

Moved by the feeling of obligation to help carry out the Master's command to preach the gospel to all nations, and by a desire to aid the most needy, the Mission Board of the United Brethren in Christ, at its first annual session, held in Westerville, Ohio, on June 1, 1854, appointed the Rev. W. J. Shuey, pastor of the First United Brethren Church of Cincinnati, as our first missionary to Africa. The executive committee of this Board soon after appointed the Rev. D. C. Kumler and the Rev. D. K. Flickinger to go also to the same field. These three sailed together from New York in January, 1855. After a sea voyage of thirty-four days, they reached Sierra Leone and landed at Freetown, February 26.

The American Missionary Association of New York had commenced, about fourteen years earlier, the Mendi Mission. Its chief stations were Good Hope, at Bonthe, on the east end of Sherbro Island and about one hundred miles south of Freetown; Kaw-Mendi, on the Jong River; and Mo-Tappan, on the Big Boom River. The Rev. George Thompson, Rev. J. S. Brooks, and Mr. D. W. Burton, Americans, were in charge of this field. To them our missionaries went with letters from New York friends. They were received with great cordiality and shown every favor possible. After making Good Hope station headquarters, and exploring the country for between two and three months for a site on which to begin mission work, Messrs. Shuey and Kumler returned to America. Mr. Flickinger continued for several months to explore the country for a location, thinking at one time to open a field on either the Big Boom or the Jong River. But without selecting a definite place, he returned to America the middle of the following May.

In June, 1856, Rev. W. B. Witt and Rev. J. K. Billheimer were appointed to go to Africa in the following December with Rev. Mr. Flickinger, who was continued superintendent of the work. They reached Freetown the following January. Mr. Flickinger went on down to Liberia to seek a location. After three weeks he returned to Sierra Leone, fully persuaded that this was to be the field of our mission work. After many efforts, assisted by Mr. D. W. Burton, of the Mendi Mission, the chief, Thomas Stephen Caulker, was induced, in March, 1857, to give a one hundred years' lease for about one hundred acres of land adjoining the town of Shaingay on the west, and located midway between Bonthe and Freetown, and occupying a cape surrounded on three sides by the ocean and about thirty feet above tide-water. On this beautiful location, one of the most healthful spots along this coast, the headquarters for our work was established. Here, finally, the mission home, the Rufus Clark and Wife Training School, the Flickinger Chapel, boys' home, parsonage, Eastborne, and minor buildings were erected, and part of the land planted in coffee trees, and a part of it continuously farmed.

As the Caulkers, from the beginning of our work to the present, have had a conspicuous part in it, the readers will be interested to know something of their history. The following facts I have learned from Mr. J. A. Cole, a native: "About the year 1750 a vessel came from England laden with goods, and brought three Englishmen, who came to seek their fortunes in West Africa. They were Messrs. Cleveland, Tucker, and Caulker. Mr. Cleveland landed at the Banana Island; Mr. S. Caulker came to the Plantain Island, and Mr. Tucker sailed southeast and settled in the country of the Gbas.

"The locality of the Plantain Island, and the property of the Caulkers (by trafficking in slaves and native products), awakened a spirit of jealousy in the Clevelands. A great enmity arose between them, which soon led to war. Mr. Cleveland collected an army and suddenly attacked the Plantain Island, and Mr. Caulker had to surrender. The island was then claimed by the Clevelands, and Mr. Caulker was removed to their headquarters on Banana Island, and employed by them. While engaged at the Banana Island, Mr. Caulker secretly used all his income in securing implements of war, and in sending presents to various chiefs in the Sherbro country, as far as the Boom, Kithin, and Bompeh rivers. This he continued for several years, until he felt he was strong enough to recover his lost estate. Then he suddenly left the Banana Island and raised an army among the Sherbros and made an attack on his rival. A single day's fight made him again master of Plantain Island. Mr. Cleveland soon after died, and Mr.

Caulker and his brother remained in control without further opposition."

The descendants of the Caulkers from that time have ruled over the Sherbros, on the coast opposite. One of the family became chief at Bompeh, and another at Shaingay. Thomas Stephen Caulker, who was chief where our mission was located at Shaingay, continued a heathen till early in the year 1871. During a meeting held by the Rev. Joseph Gomer, this chief was converted, and died a Christian on the 28th of August following. Some of his children had been converted before their father, and the family have been faithful friends and supporters of our missions for over a quarter of a century.

The Caulkers, as stated above, are of English blood on the paternal side, a few generations back, while on the maternal side they are of Sherbro ancestry. This is also true of the Tuckers and many others on the west coast of Africa. But it is not always safe to infer the lineage from the English name they bear. The natives are fond of getting a new name of foreign origin. Many of the children in the mission schools bear the names of patrons in America; others bear English names for the same reason. It is very amusing to hear the names some of the people have given themselves, such as "Pepper Sauce," "Two Copper," "Pipe of Tobacco," "Bottle of Beer," "Mashed Potatoes," etc.

From the beginning the Sherbro Mission has been carried forward by a succession of faithful and most worthy men and women, and the work has prospered in their hands.

On October 21, 1875, at a convention held in Dayton, Ohio, the Woman's Missionary Association of the United Brethren in Christ was organized, and at once became an efficient co-worker with the General Board of Missions in carrying forward the enterprise in Africa. They located their headquarters at Rotufunk, about fifty miles east of Freetown on the Bompeh River. The work of this station was begun in the autumn of 1877, by Miss Emily Becken, who at the end of nineteen months was succeeded by Mrs. M. M. Mair, and has since been followed by others equally noble and devoted, whose labors have been blessed and prospered abundantly. At this center of the work of the Woman's Missionary Association there is a chapel, high-school building, home for the missionaries, girls' home, boys' home, a workshop, and a storehouse—all good buildings of wood and stone. They had employed in this field, the first of May, 1898, eight Americans, two of whom were physicians, one a mechanic, and five were teachers or pastors; also eight native pastors and teachers. These were employed at twelve different circuits or stations. Some of these circuits included forty towns and villages where services were held, and new fields were being entered continually by these zealous workmen.

About the beginning of the year 1883, the American Missionary Association, of New York, which had carried on the Mendi Mission since 1841, turned the same over to our Board. Their two chief stations were Good Hope, at Bonthe, where there was a good chapel, school-house, residence, and a tract of land now in the city of

Bonthe; and Avery, where there was a good chapel, residence, sawmill, and a coffee farm; a farm at Kaw-Mendi and one at Mo-Tappan were included.

The transfer of these stations, and their equipment, and nearly $40,000 in money for their maintenance, brought new responsibilities and enlarged our field.

The American Missionary Association had become discouraged over the meager returns, and wishing to engage mission work elsewhere, after an expenditure of $300,000 (so I was informed), and the death of many of their workmen, they kindy transferred all their African interests to us. About this same time $13,000 was received from the Freedman's Mission Aid Society of London, England, through the influence and services of the Rev. D. K. Flickinger, who was for over thirty years connected, more or less intimately with, and rendered distinguished service in, this field of work.

The work of converting the natives was very slow for many years. Thomas Tucker was the first convert. He was found, and brought to the mission in 1857, a raw heathen. The superintendent, Rev. J. K. Billheimer, who with his noble wife served this mission most ably for many years, employed Thomas as a laborer, and afterwards as boat-captain. He was honest and trustworthy, but slow in grasping the plan of salvation. The exact date of his conversion is not known, but in 1870, when Mr. Gomer and wife came to this field, Thomas was greatly aroused and made a fuller consecration of himself to God. Mr. Gomer pushed him forward in religious services, especially after the organization of our first African church, in 1875. He became very influential with Chief Caulker, who made Mr. Tucker a sub-chief over a large district. In 1885 he died, after having been a preacher of the gospel for the two years prior to his decease. He lived a good life and was widely influential.

Lucy Caulker was another one of the earliest converts. She was a daughter of the old chief, and was opposed in her early Christian life, but maintained her integrity, and finally saw her father and most of his family converted. She and her sisters, and her brother, Chief Thomas Neal Caulker, and many of the children, have become members of the church at Shaingay. The chief acted as my interpreter the last time I preached in Shaingay Chapel.

From small beginnings, and after years of discouragement, the work suddenly sprang forward, wide revivals followed, and now over 6,000 souls have had their names placed on church records, most of whom, it is believed, are converted to God from their former heathenism. The work has spread from Shaingay in the west to Mongherri in the east; and from Rokell in the north to Bonthe in the south. Of course, the whole of this region is not occupied, but its conquest is under way. In the persons of the missionaries and their converts, new ideals of life are working their silent but certain transformations of character. In the word of God read and preached, a light has dawned, the morning star of a day of hope for this long benighted people. In the literary and industrial schools established, many noble young men and women have already been trained, the first-fruits, the earnest of a great host ransomed from their former degradation.

The following are the assignments of the workmen to their several fields, made at the annual conference held in Shaingay, January 1, 2, 1898. Bompeh District is the part under the Woman's Missionary Association; Sherbro-Mendi District is the field occupied by the General Board of Missions:

Bompeh District—I. N. Cain, P. E.

Rotufunk Station—Dr. Mary E. Archer, pastor.

Rotufunk School—Miss F. M. Cronise, principal; Miss Minnie Eaton, Mrs. M. M. Cain, and J. Weaver, teachers.

Rotufunk Girls' Home—Miss Ella Schenck, matron.

Rotufunk Industrial Department—A. A. Ward.

Rotufunk Medical Department—Dr. Mary Archer.

River Circuit—A. A. Ward, assisted by pupils of Rotufunk School.

Rotufunk Circuit—J. Dodds.

Palli Circuit—J. B. W. Johnson.

Bompeh Circuit—To be supplied.

Masimera Circuit—To be supplied.

Makundo Circuit—T. F. Hallowell.

Mongherri Circuit—George Keister.

Kwallu Circuit—Mrs. J. Thompson.

Somanasogo School—J. Dodds.

Taiama—Rev. and Mrs. L. A. McGrew.

Taiama Medical Department—Dr. M. Hatfield.

Taiama Itinerant—I. Inskip.

Sherbro-Mendi District—L. O. Burtner, P. E.

Avery Station and Circuit—F. S. Minshall; C. A. Remmie and J. E. Hughes, assistants.

Avery School—Myrtle Minshall; Laura Remmie, assistant.

Good Hope Station—R. C. Taylor; F. A. Anthony, assistant.

Good Hope School—A. T. Sumner, T. A. Davis, and Mrs. Jane Randall.

Daymah Circuit—E. C. Bickersteth.

Otterbein Circuit—J. A. Evans; assistant to be supplied.

Jehovah Circuit—H. J. Williams.

Mano (Mendi) Circuit—C. A. Columbus.

Damballah Circuit—S. B. Morrison.

Mandoh Circuit—Not supplied.

Shaingay Circuit—A. T. Howard.

Shaingay School—A. T. Howard, principal; May S. Howard, A. T. Caulker, and Henry Evans, assistants.

Superintendent of Boys' and Girls' Home—Mrs. L. O. Burtner.

Rembee—G. R. Woolsley.

Mocobo—Stephen B. Caulker.

Work to be arranged for Kezia Funkhouser.

Besides the houses and their equipment at the above-named stations, the General Board has eleven farms, of 100 to 160 acres each. They are located at Shaingay, Mambo, Rembee, Kooloong, Mufus, Tonkola, Mocobo, Charmany, Avery, Bonthe, Kaw-Mendi, and Mo-Tappan. The Woman's Association has farms of about the same size at Rotufunk, Palli, Rokon, Kwallu, and Taiama. These farms were given by the native chiefs, as a contribution toward the support of missions and schools. They have never yet been fully utilized but they are capable of furnishing a revenue, as well as becoming model farms to teach the natives better methods of agriculture.

Besides these farms, the mission property here, owned by the General Board, is estimated at $55,000; and an expenditure has been made in this field by the same Board, of nearly $300,000, besides an equal amount expended by the American Missionary Association, before transferring their Mendi Mission to us. The permament property of the Woman's Board is given in their last report at $17,000, and their expenditures in this field have been $101,316.26.

The most valuable assets of the mission are its faithful missionaries, American and native; its converts; its trained young men and women; and the good seed sown in the hearts of many thousands of natives who are not yet saved.

CHAPTER IV.

DIFFICULTIES TO BE MET.

It is unwise to conceal, or to ignore the difficulties in any undertaking. This is very true concerning the field of which I write, for in many things to be forewarned is to be forearmed.

1. **The Climate** is unfriendly to the white man. The extreme, continuous heat and moisture cause rapid growth and decay of vegetation, and this, added to the sluggish streams and numerous ponds and mangrove swamps covered several feet deep with fetid mud, along the flat coast regions, fills the air with malarial poison, and the breathing of this air is sooner or later followed by African, or malarial fever. Not much is fully known of the nature of this fever. The physicians generally say that the malarial microbes act on the red corpuscles, leaving nothing of them but the dark pigment found in the skin and organs of malarial subjects; that the microbes appear at the commencement of an attack of fever, and increase in quantity as the fever increases, and decrease as it decreases; and that by examining the blood they are able fairly well to tell how many remissions may be expected, and to judge of the severity of the case; which, with the knowledge that quinine only effects malarial microbes at a certain stage of their existence, is helpful in treatment.

The natives do not suffer much from this fever. Their constant, and to us excessive, use of red pepper in their food evidently helps to prevent it. Their easy, slow movement, rarely becoming fatigued, is also favorable to resisting the fever. When they do take it, they use a tea made from a native herb, and soon recover. (This "fever plant" of the natives should receive attention from the whites.)

I suffered of this fever in less than three months after reaching Africa, but this was due to sleeping on the rivers in an open boat, wading through swamps, and overworking.

Our mission has lost a fewer number of persons (four in all) from sickness than any other class of foreigners of equal numbers. This is due to the superior persons, and the more complete obedience to sanitary laws, as well as a kind Providence. By obedience to the following conditions our people may continue to have comparative immunity from the ravages of this fever: Avoid all liquors; boil all drinking water; learn the proper use of quinine; avoid all chill, if possible; avoid over-exertion and worry; eat the evening meal at from 6 to 7 o'clock, and before starting out in the morning have a good cup of tea or coffee, and bread and butter; eat much red pepper with the food; perfectly trust that Providence that guards the sparrow, and much more cares for his children; and visit Mt. Leicester, and home, when necessary.

2. **The Mode of Travel** is another difficulty in this region. Horses cannot live here Some say the natives, who get their living by hammock-carrying, poison them; others say the tsetse fly destroys them; while the probable fact is, that entozoa kill them. Across the country the hammock

is the only conveyance. The hammock is slung to a pole of bamboo or to a sawed scantling, and a board three feet long is fastened to each end. The traveler sits, or reclines, in the hammock, which hangs under the pole, and the boards rest on the heads of four natives. The paths are frequently too narrow for the hammock, or they cross rough places or over a stream bridged by a foot-log— in any of these cases the traveler must descend and walk. If the stream is wide, a "dugout" canoe is the means of transit; or if it is a wide pond, the traveler mounts upon the shoulders of a big black man, who carries him over. I was once carried two hundred yards through water four feet deep in this manner, and on the trip I laughed heartily to think how funny it would be if the black carrier should fall and give me a bath.

Our stations lie over one hundred miles along the ocean coast, and the mode of travel in this case is most frequently in a sail-and-row-boat, as here it is rarely convenient to take a steamer on the ocean, and never possible up and down the rivers. The contrary wind, the opposing tide, the sudden tornado of violent wind, flashing lightning, roaring thunder, and deluging rain, and the frightened, panic-stricken native oarsmen are not easily described.

3 Add to these the continuous heat, absence of home friends, and the worry incident to dealing with the natives, and one will know some of the difficulties which wear out the vital forces of the missionary. I here present a paper written by Mrs. Zella B. King, one of our missionaries, which presents well the

"DANGERS AND DIFFICULTIES OF MISSIONARY LIFE.

"The life of a missionary is one of varied experiences. At times everything seems bright and hopeful, and again there seems to be much that is dark and discouraging. Sometimes there is a ready response to all his efforts, and the changing scenes and conditions add interest to his life. At other times his sowing promises little fruitage and his daily duties become monotonous and dull.

"Civilization has produced many conveniences that we cannot have in Africa. One of the first inconveniences the missionary must meet after arriving is that of travel. He has been accustomed to be carried over the land in comfortable railway trains. Here, many of the journeys must be made by sea in boats propelled by oars and sails. The boat moves so slowly at times against wind and current that days are required to make a journey of a hundred miles. At times the sea is as calm as a summer lake, and again it is so wild and furious that we think our little boat will be buried in the deep.

"On land we must either walk or be carried in hammocks. At first one feels unwilling to be carried thus, and see the strong-muscled men puffing and sweating to relieve you of the fatigue of walking. One never seems so heavy to himself as when he sits in a hammock and sees the hard boards resting on the heads of men, and hears them panting up the steep places. It is trying to one's feeling of independence and self-respect. But these men are accustomed to the work and glad for the opportunity of earning a few pence. It is necessary also to save ourselves whenever possible if we hope to live long in this climate. The newcomer must learn also to care for his health. The land is so beautiful that it is hard to realize it is filled with malaria, but it is too true. There are few whom the fever does not attack. In our own mission we have been very fortunate in this respect. Although we have not been free from fevers, yet we have suffered less than others.

"A missionary, to keep well and happy here, must learn to possess his soul in patience, or he will soon be worn out by the cares and worries of everyday life. He must expect things to move slowly and his plans often to be disturbed. He must be willing to await results, for one of the greatest obstacles has been the total indifference to spiritual things, which the heathen everywhere evinces. It sometimes seems that the labor has been in vain, but He who has bidden us 'go' will care for his own. It is ours but to be faithful to the task he has assigned us.

"I have been asked to give some personal experiences and mention some of the difficulties we have had. As we look back over the three years spent in this colony we remember a few dark days. But there has never been a day so dark that there has not been a gleam of sunshine. There have been times when it was necessary that some sacrifices be made and a few dangers encountered, but His strength has always been sufficient.

"Among some of our personal difficulties are *separation, with limited means of communication.* During the last eighteen months Mr. King has been absent from home one-half the time. For weeks together I have not been able to hear from him. To remember the dangers on the sea, the deadly climate with its fevers, which so frequently strike down the victims in a few days, the exposure to rains, and the poor houses in which he must often lodge, is a trial which drives one to the dear Saviour for comfort.

"We had another trial, with burglars. Once in Bonthe, when alone, I awoke in the night with the sound of some one in my room. When I looked I discovered a man at a trunk, beginning to help himself. He was naked, so as to be less incumbered if discovered, and also had a weapon of defense. He did not leave the room until I arose and went toward him. Following him to the window through which he had entered, I saw his companion outside. Thieves disturb in America, but here the restraint of law is slight and the heathen mind is cruel and savage.

"There are many little annoyances in dealing with the people, that wear on a person. The heathen by nature are childlike and dependent. They are forgetful, and without fixed moral principles to govern them. They are creatures of impulse. They imagine a missionary can settle all difficulties, hence he has to hear many unpleasant things between persons.

"We have been in some very heavy storms on the sea in our little boat, and once when very ill, were a day and a night under a heavy rain; so that we consider it nothing less than a kind Providence that intervened. It makes the Father more real to us to feel that he stretches out his arm and saves his children from special danger. One feels ashamed to mention these trials when we remember how freely his grace is given. 'Most gladly therefore will I rather glory in my infirmities, that the power of Christ may rest upon me. Therefore I take pleasure in infirmities, in reproaches, in necessities, in persecutions, in distresses for Christ's sake: for when I am weak, then am I strong.' "

CHAPTER V.

MECHANICAL, AGRICULTURAL, AND MEDICAL WORK.

To the careful observer the mission that expends its whole effort to secure the conversion of the heathen is making a mistake. It is also a mistake to educate them in a knowledge of books merely. The natives here have good memories and large imitativeness, and hence learn to read and write with great ease. This is always in danger of inflating their vanity. One of the evils of the Mohammedan teacher is that he plays upon this vanity of the native, by making him believe that he is a "bookman," when he can barely read and write.

There are now as many clerks as are needed for the civil service in Sierra Leone. Every native who has some education is in danger of thinking that this entitles him to get a living without doing any manual labor. Hence, the most urgent need in this field is to combine with religious and literary teaching technical training of such a character as will make manual labor honorable in the eyes of the natives. Slavery, of course, has made labor dishonorable, but it can be made honorable by making it possible to do the work in a superior fashion.

The native's method of farming is very rude, and he produces only what supplies, in the most limited manner his daily wants. The soil is productive and yields a generous return. The native hoe, ax, and cutlass must be supplanted by better implements, not the best known to us, but better than they know now. Our farms there should be used to show the natives how best to raise cassava, corn, rice, vegetables, cotton, coffee, tea, bananas, pineapples, oranges, limes, native cherries, "Bundoo fruit," and other native fruits, plants, and vines.

The man who will teach the natives how to yoke the ox and train him to the plow and the cart and the saddle will confer an unspeakable favor. The raising of cattle, sheep, and goats for food and export may become an important industry, as well as a help to elevate the natives, by engaging them in honest toil.

Quite as important is it to teach them how to utilize the iron, stone, clay, and timber. Iron ore is abundant, but only the simplest tools are made in the country. Clay is found for pottery or bricks, but only a few rude pots are produced. Timber is good and abundant, but it is utilized only in a primitive way. We must teach the youth how to handle and take care of the mattock, hoe, ax, hammer, hatchet, saw, adz, chisel, and auger, and the lathe; and how to make nails, knives, forks, spoons, plates, etc.; also improved methods of spinning, weaving, cutting and making clothes, as well as how to cook and serve a wider and better variety of food. This will take time, men, and money; but it will tell more for civilization, and for making permanent the religious work than all the book knowledge possible. Do not diminish the latter kind of knowledge, but increase the mechanical and agricultural kind.

I have heard Governor Cardew express himself earnestly in favor of industrial education for the natives.

The Right Rev. E. G. Ingham, D. D., former Bishop of Sierra Leone, and for many years a resident of Freetown, is very emphatic on this subject. He says:

"Experience is daily proving to those who have eyes to see, that the peculiar past history of this race demands special consideration on the part of those who aspire to educate. Any failure, for instance, to realize the irresponsibility of the lot of the slave, the utter barrenness of his surroundings, the license into which liberty would tend to degenerate, or the disgust at manual labor that would naturally characterize the newly emancipated, would be fatal to the adoption of suitable methods of training. When the missionary receives under his care a youth who has been living under the patriarchial system of domestic slavery, and whose fathers before him were slaves, when he puts clothes on his body, and a book in one hand, he should, unless he courts failure, put a tool in the other.

"What we would press upon the attention of our educationalists is simply this: That every elementary or higher grade school should have its technical department, however small; that it should be under a well-trained European Christian mechanic, who should have some three or four manual trades in his fingers; *that this should be definite Christian work;* that the technical class should be as compulsory, as much a part of the school curriculum as the scripture or the grammar lesson; that every boy should have a course of training in carpentering, turning, forging, etc., quite irrespective of the particular part for which he is being trained. It is evident that the break thus created in the monotonous round of daily study must be a great relief, and tend to quicken apprehension, and there is abundant room for these classes in the school regime of each day."

This quotation contains profound wisdom. The course here recommended would develop the mechanical genius, of which the natives, by lack of use, are notably deficient; it would also fit them for some useful pursuit.

Some instruction in medicine should be given in some one of our African schools. It need not be a full course in order to be very helpful where physicians are so scarce and where the witch-doctor is the chief resort in case of sickness. The following letter from Doctor Archer, at Rotufunk, will indicate the work of a medical missionary in this region:

"During the past two years in Africa I have treated hundreds of patients with varying shades of diseases, from the 'chigger,' in the small boy's toe to smallpox and tertiary syphilis. We have an office and dispensary where patients come regularly every morning for treatment, for which a small fee is charged (varying from one shilling to one pound per month, according to the nature and severity of the case). Some are covered with sores from head to foot.

"I have two assistants, a boy and a girl, who help wash and dress the patients' sores and attend to their bodily ailments in general.

"Every morning, after their physical ills are administered to, the patients assemble in the office, some seated on benches and chairs, while others are seated on the floor, where they eagerly listen while we read and interpret the Scriptures to them, teaching them mainly of the life of Christ and of the plan of salvation; sometimes we use our Sunday-School Bible Lesson Charts to illustrate the lesson, as they can grasp the thoughts better when they can see the illustrated picture, which they are very eager for when a new one is presented.

"Many of them come from 'up country,' several days' journey, and have never heard of the Son of God. Jesus Christ is a strange name to them. Often Mohammedans come with their false ideas, and here in the medical department for the first time in their lives they listen to the story of the cross, and when I tell them that Jesus loves them in their sickness and miserable condition, they say, 'I am so glad to hear that word.'

"One woman, after having been cured, said 'When I first came to you for treatment, I did not believe a word you said about this religion of Jesus Christ, but when I found that you could cure my sickness, and now my sores are healed, I believe it all, and now I am so glad I have accepted this sweet religion.'

"The people are very superstitious regarding their sickness They think their disease, of whatever nature, is due to a witch—either some enemy has witched them or they themselves are guilty of witchcraft. Sometimes they think they have unwittingly offended one of their numerous devils and that he is angry with them, and they have 'pulled plenty sacrifice' to the devil before coming to me for treatment. These devil sacrifices consist in a ceremony of pouring water for the devils, placing for him some choice rice or other food, sacrificing animals, erecting a long pole with a white rag tied to the top near the 'devil house' (which protects almost every town), or at the entrance of the 'devil bush.' They also beg their ancestors to intercede for them, etc.

"When these devices fail to appease the wrath of the devil, and when the 'country doctor' with his magical arts and charms and his boiled leaves and roots, over which he has 'pulled magic,' fail, the afflicted ones come to us, saying, 'The witch done catch me bad.'

"We first try to relieve their minds of the witch idea and plant a seed of Christianity, which is often choked by these superstitious ideas which have been handed down from generation to generation.

"I assure them that their disease has a natural cause, and that instead of praying to their ancestors and the devil, who cannot help them, they should pray to Jesus Christ, who so loved them that he gave his life for them, and as we kneel together in prayer for them their voices may be heard saying, 'Ye pa yi!' (So let it be.) Thus they are praying to the true God; their hearts are reaching out after something better than they have known. Oh for more consecrated workers to lead these minds and hearts, which are just ready to be molded, to the great 'Fountain of healing.' 'The harvest truly is great.'

"The people forsake even their immediate

friends when they become sick. Husbands abandon their wives, and wives their husbands, when they become disabled. What love existed in health seems to die when one becomes sick or helpless, and they often say, 'Makie die one time,' that is, let the sick one die at once; and if he lingers with sickness, they say, 'He can humbug plenty.' Yet when he dies the whole neighborhood sets up a wail which is prolonged for several days, according to the rank of the deceased. If a 'big man' dies, the people fire guns, drink rum, 'pull big eat,' dance, etc., which continues for days and even weeks and months.

"We hope to have a hospital soon, so that when patients are brought down from the interior we can have a place, with the proper sanitary conditions, to care for them; but at the present, patients are brought several days' journey in hammocks and placed in a native mud house with little or no care, no nurse or attendant but possibly a slave child.

"I call to mind one woman thus brought, and when I made my morning visits after office hours I would find the woman, in a nude condition, lying on the earth floor, without even a straw mat under her or a country cloth over her, with sometimes a rough stick under her head as a kind of pillow, the stick being left over from a fire made in the middle of the room, by the child attendant, the previous night.

"If a heavy rain fell during the night or day it would beat into the house and soak the ground, when, if the woman had strength enough, she would crawl out to a dry place in some corner; if not, she would remain in the mud and water. Sometimes she would tell me through my interpreter that she had had nothing to eat for a whole day. I would give her a dose of medicine and leave her in the hands of God, for no person was there to whom I could commit the charge, and hasten on to another case in almost the same condition.

"Another case is that of a man, who, I am informed, had been sick for seven years and had not taken a step for more than a year, having rheumatism with some complications. He was brought here from a distant town and given quarters in the home of his friends. He had but very little attention from his people, but was able to take the medicine left him, without any assistance. He often had food but once in twenty-four hours, and I often went in and found his mat and country cloth, his only articles of bedding, soaked with the rain which had beaten in through the rude window or the open bamboo roof, and occasionally found him crouched in one corner which seemed to be drier than the rest. As soon as the man had recovered sufficiently he cooked rice or cassava for himself. After about three months' treatment, with these unfavorable conditions, the man was able to walk a half mile with little fatigue. With favorable conditions he would have recovered much sooner.

"In another dark house I went through two or three dark, damp rooms (on the walls of which a low-grade of vegetation was springing up) to a little back room, dark, damp, moldy, and filthy, with sickening odors so strong that I was compelled to hasten out into the air and sunshine, for which I thanked the dear Lord. In this little back room a woman lay on a rude kind of bed, 'sick unto death.'

"She was the only occupant of the house. Some days the people would carry her food and some days she had none. It is not necessary to add that she soon crossed over.

"Anxious for the physical and spiritual condition of these people, I long for the time when the 'Son of righteousness' shall arise with healing in his wings over this great moral canker of heathenism."

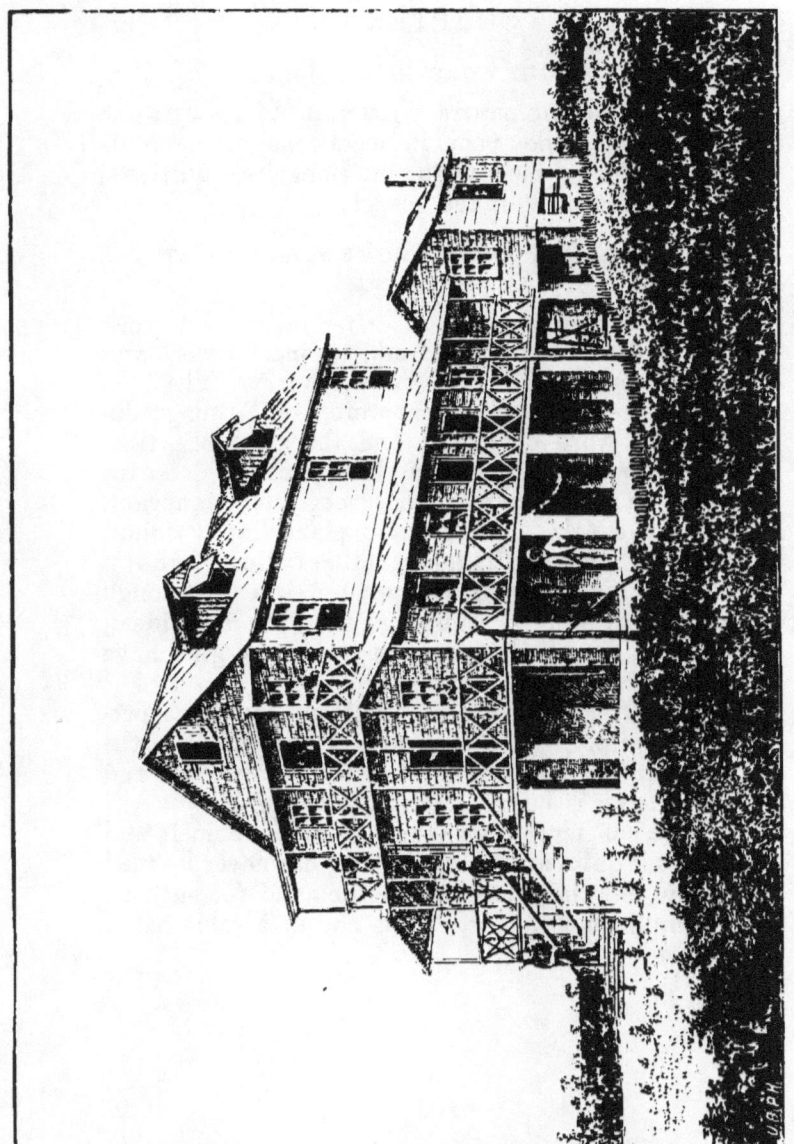

Mary Sowers Home for Girls.

CHAPTER VI.

SOME WORK BEING DONE.

The following papers, written in Africa by those whose names they bear, indicate some of the kinds of work being done by our missionaries, additional to the preaching of the gospel:

"THE MARY SOWER'S HOME FOR GIRLS, AT ROTUFUNK.

"For a number of years after missionary work was undertaken at Rotufunk, no special work was carried on for the girls of the country. The field was large and the laborers were few. But gradually the work developed and there came a time when it was felt that something must be done for these bits of humanity, these neglected, ignorant, immortal girls. Prayers and plans finally culminated in a commodious, homelike building, known as the Mary Sower's Home for Girls. Although conditions and surroundings here are not ideal, they are far in advance of anything the girls have known.

"When a child enters the Home, without previous contact with civilization or knowledge of the English language, communication between her and the matron is largely restricted to signs.

"She has never been taught to clothe herself and thinks it quite unnecessary. She has never learned to sew, for there has been no demand for such an accomplishment. Never has she at a table eaten her simple meal of rice, having been quite content to sit down on the ground and eat with her hand from the iron pot in which the rice has been cooked. Why should she use a spoon when she has washed her hands? Probably she takes the same view as did an old heathen man who, looking askance at an Englishman eating with knife and fork, said that his hands must be very dirty since he would not eat with them.

"She has been taught to believe that witches, ghosts, evil spirits, devils, and many more wonderful things have power to harm her. The superstitions and credulities of the country have tinged and warped her life. In the country dances she early learned to take a part, and the country songs, with their questionable sentiments, have been absorbed into her child life.

"Recently, two children about five years of age were admitted to the Home; one, Temni, the other, Mendi; as bright and promising as can be obtained. At that early age they knew dozens of these songs and numerous dances, and were already familiar with evils of which many adult minds at home are ignorant. When they were told that these amusements were not allowed, they evidently disapproved of our taste. But what wonder! They are taught nothing better.

"When, in the providence of God, a girl is brought to the mission, a brighter day dawns for her, and infinite possibilities are placed within her grasp. The Home has been open now about ten years, and in that time about thirty girls have been admitted for longer or shorter terms. When a girl is given to us, her parents or guardians sign a paper, renouncing all claim to her, including the right to give her in marriage. On our side, we agree to keep her until she is of age, or until she marries, provided she behaves well. It has been difficult at times to obtain suitable girls, for which several reasons may be given: Prevailing sentiment teaches that female education is unnecessary. We do not desire those who have been initiated into the secret societies, as their influence would largely counteract our best efforts. After receiving word that some benevolent person at home wishes to name and educate a girl, considerable time may elapse before the demand can be supplied. Among those taken, there has been a gradual sifting process, some having been found to be incompetent or unworthy of the great gift of Christian training within their reach.

"Marked advancement is seen in most of those who have remained several years. They are taught such things as will be of practical use when they go out to make homes for themselves, as sewing, washing, ironing, and housework of various sorts. There is a market value for this kind of work in the colony, so they will be able to make their own living if necessary. But one thought in training them is that they may become the wives of our native workers, and together establish Christian homes. Some have already done this, and the contrast between these homes and those of their people is appreciable.

"Some have a desire to tell their people of the new hope that has entered their lives since they came into contact with gospel influences. When they go to their homes for vacation, the Bible is taken along and read as opportunities arise. Frequently on Sunday morning they go out two by two to the nearer towns and hold short services, which seem to be acceptable. It has been encouraging to see the older girls, one by one, take upon themselves the vows of the church.

"A special providence has seemed to preside over the Home, for only once has the death angel crossed the threshold. Little Laura Meredith quickly succumbed to an acute form of smallpox. She was a good, obedient child, and although she had been but a short time an inmate of the Home, had doubtless received sufficient light to guide her through the pearly gates to her Father's home.

"The one in charge of the Home has a very great responsibility resting upon her, for largely to her hands is given the molding of the destiny of these untaught children. The work is exacting, and detrimental to the nervous system, hence the term of service cannot be very lengthy. Five Christian women have given their best efforts in behalf of this cause. There have been discouragements and seeming failures, but there have also been encouragements and successes. Eternity alone will reveal the results of the seed sown."—*Minnie Eaton.*

"THE CLARK TRAINING SCHOOL.

"Missionaries in different foreign fields have different opinions as to the grade of schools that ought to be supported with mission funds. Though this question cannot be definitely settled, it is generally concluded that elementary schools, at least, ought to be maintained. The founders of our own mission realized in the very beginning that schools established in various places would give a permanency to their efforts that could be attained in no other way.

"By the daily contact of teacher with pupil education has proved a valuable means of instilling the truth of the gospel into young minds. Satan, ever alert, and not so stupid as to neglect his influence over these little ones, finds in every mind good soil for the growth of superstition and love for wickedness. While he is thus beguiling the young into the secret societies and other evil practices of a heathen country, let the children of light not be unmindful of their opportunity of drawing these boys and girls away from their native superstitions and filling their minds with stories more pure than those rehearsed in the mysterious bush. It is not difficult in any neighborhood to gather the children into school. True it is that many are sent rather that they may learn the English language than that they may be taught the Word of God, because the advantage of understanding the white man's tongue is apparent, where the value of the way of life is unknown.

"At present there are advanced schools in Shaingay and Bonthe, while primary work is being done among the children of Avery, Dama, Kooloong, Yorbofor, and Mandoh. The Clark Training School, erected in 1877, through the benevolence of Africa's true friends, Mr. and Mrs. Rufus Clark, of Denver, Colo., was at first intended only as a theological school and boys' domitory. However, since this splendid structure was so very commodious, it was soon made to serve a broader purpose without in the least interfering with the original design. Hence all the grades were placed in the same building and under the same management, and now six of the rooms, including the library, are used for school purposes. The library, of about 650 volumes, to which Mr. Hulitt generously contributed $300, and to which Bishop Mills and others have made extensive additions, is daily used by the students and missionaries.

"The course of study in the Training School, as now arranged, consists, besides the elementary branches, of English and general history, physical geography, rhetoric, physiology, astronomy, physics, one year of Latin, and a part of the Bible normal course. Furthermore, a regular plan of Bible study is laid out for all grades. The younger pupils memorize certain psalms and portions of the New Testament, and the teaching is thus continued until these children in Bible knowledge easily equal the boys and girls of their own age in other countries. During the past year there were enrolled in the Clark Training School 158 pupils. Three of these, one young woman and two young men, are soon to graduate and will be employed by our mission as teachers. There are other promising young people who within a few years can finish their courses of study. Unfortunate it is, however, that the ideas of the parents and guardians of these children have not been sufficiently broadened to appreciate the merits of a high educational standard. Consequently, in many cases, one who has completed the third or fourth reader is considered so far ahead of his unlettered companions that he is taken from school and placed in some position where he can earn a little money.

RUFUS CLARK AND WIFE THEOLOGICAL SCHOOL.

Nevertheless, it is but just to state that some of these students who have enjoyed the advantages of school for only a short time have coupled with their meager education a commendable zeal, and have become substantial members of the church.

"In the last ten years, eighteen of the young people of the Training School have become teachers and itinerants in our own mission, and two more are employed by other churches, while four young men are in the employ of the government, and seven are in mercantile pursuits. Of this number twelve are at present with our mission and doing creditable work. It is a matter of keen regret that young men are sometimes induced to leave the mission work because of the larger salaries offered by merchants or the government, and all praise is due these consecrated students who decline lucrative positions for the sake of giving their own people the bread of life.

"If we may forecast the future from the experience of the past, the greater number will not lack that consecration What will be the direct effect of these classes annually graduated from the Training School, trained to respect God's law as revealed in his Word, in their own bodies, in every plant or wind or wave or tide, and sent out openly to live a lawful life among people who know no cause but the caprice of witch or devil, the Master himself knows who sent his disciples forth to teach all nations. The registers of His school are carefully kept. Believing that in the summaries at the end of the age, the Clark Training School will be found to share, we are glad to labor and to wait."—*May S. Howard.*

Miss Florence M. Cronise, A.M., left a professorship of modern languages in Otterbein University to go to Rotufunk as principal of the high school While doing most efficient work in the school-room, she has been studying the language, myths, and traditions of the natives. The following is from her pen:

" LANGUAGES AND FOLK-LORE OF SIERRA LEONE.

"For little more than a century the English have laid a colonist's claim to the peninsula of Sierra Leone. Immediately upon acquiring possession they transferred to it 1,100 descendants of free negroes, who before the American war of 1776 had been landed proprietors, and whose fealty to England and disloyalty to the Stars and Stripes had made them penniless wanderers. With these settlers were Foulahs and Mandingoes, who were Mohammedans of various nations increased by members of a few African tribes, proselyted from devil worship to the tenets of the Koran. Mingled with all these were European fortune hunters. The great mass of the population of the colony, not classed with the foregoing, were either liberated slaves or their descendants. British seamen have rescued from the pestilential atmosphere of French, Spanish, and Portuguese slave-ships, chained, tortured human beings, and placed them, free citizens, on British soil. In 1811 the population of the colony numbered 45,000, more than half of whom were liberated slaves. Between 1819 and 1833, 27,167 slaves had been liberated and and landed in Sierra Leone, where, in 1842, about forty African tribes were represented. These when landed were complete savages, each tribe having its own more or less developed language, which amid the new surroundings had suddenly become an insufficient vehicle of thought. The present population of the colony is computed at 480,000, and over seventy languages are said to be spoken in Freetown, a city of 40,000 inhabitants. Each native tongue, with slight commingling of Spanish, French, and Portuguese, has tinged and corrupted the commonly acquired English, making of it Pidgin-English, that is, business English, which the mother tongue would scorn to own. Some of the tribal languages die out, yet to a considerable degree in Freetown, and almost universally in the Hinterland, native languages do and will prevail. Naturally, the policy of the ruling government is to disseminate the English language with English law throughout its possessions; nevertheless, missionaries of that and other nations advocate a speaking, teaching, preaching knowledge of the tribal dialects on their fields of labor. This is necessary in order to gain direct and satisfactory communication between speaker and hearer. Rarely can an interpreter be found who forms a capable and conscientious connecting link. Only by this language-getting can the most vital understanding and outgrowing sympathy exist; only thus can those who have juvenile minds in training enter well into their mode of thought and follow their process of reasoning. Missionary annals record the greatest soul-winning among those who through earnest labor have made a strange unwritten tongue their own, reduced it to writing, and used it in translating the Scriptures. Children with receptive brain and ready memory can probably best be trained through the English language, with its wealth of text-books, but their parents must be reached through the dialect they understand, or they will not be reached at all. A lesser argument in favor of language acquisition is the mental culture it affords the missionary, who feels justified in such study when he would begrudge it in lines further removed from his loved and chosen work. Constant mental outlay demands mental refreshment, which is too often disregarded. Unfortunately the average missionary finds himself so cumbered with a multiplicity of cares that, however strong an advocate he may be of language study, he must replace the quiet hours he craves with immediately pressing tasks, and his curtailed reading is chiefly in the Book of books.

"About the year 1800 a Scotch missionary, Mr. Brunton, acquired the Soosoo language, and prepared a grammar, vocabulary, spelling-book, catechism, three dialogues on Christianity, and an abridgement of Scripture history and doctrine. This was the first attempt ever made to reduce a language of western Africa to writing. In 1866 Rev. William Schlenker had a part of the Old Testament and all of the New translated into Temni, and ready for publication; and in 1871 the four Gospels, Acts, and Romans, translated into Mendi, came from the press. There is also a primer, a reader, a grammar, and a dictionary in Mendi, and the same in Temni. Into the latter Rev. Mr. Alley, of the Church Missionary Society, translated the Pentateuch and some other writings. Sherbro is spoken throughout a strip of coast which extends southward from the Bompeh River, and includes Shaingay and Sherbro Island. Being unwritten, its acquisition is more difficult than that of the Mendi, which is, in the same localities, almost universally understood. The Church Missionary Society is employing native languages in its interior schools, and foreign teachers have no work assigned them on first reaching the field, other than learning the dialects they are to use. These primitive languages, like others, abound in figures of speech and pithy parables, but are limited in scope. The loftiest sentiments of Scripture are expressed with difficulty and circumlocution, because the untaught aborigine has no conception of them, and language never wells from springs higher than the most exalted thought of those it serves.

"Africa locks her history in the breast of a sphinx, the stony heart of a pyramid, or beneath the shifting desert sands, and the silence of aeons of time holds the key. What bits of tradition are extant are spun into the warp and woof of the web of the spider, who becomes himself the hero of tales of war and peace, superstitious worship, devils, and vaguest notions of a life to come. To him are ascribed all cunning, sleeplessness, and well-nigh immortality, the belief being current that from all dangers his charmed life must escape. Uncle Remus's tales find here their ancestry, 'Bra Rabbit' being nearly identical with 'Conie' Rabbit, and a companion in adventures of Mr. Spider These quaint stories are so like those of India and South America as to suggest a common origin. The following are bits of the folk-lore with which the African continent is rife:

'DE SPIDER AN DE PEOPLE WHAY DEY WALKER.

'One tem na one country, de chief bin wan make big dinner, so he sen fo all dem people fo cum, an he tell de people say, wen den dey come, make den bring plenty cow. Befo den dey come de chief hesef kill plenty cow an say: "Who go bring big pot. I go gie um one cow." So Spider say he go bring de pot. Wen he bring um de chief gie um one cow, an he kill dis cow an he yeat de cow *all*, but he no yeat de head. So he take de head, he go na da road whay den people go pas wid den cow, an he dig one hole na middle road, an he put dis cow he head dey. But he no put all, so dat if pusson draw um he no go be hard fo pull um dey. He tie rope to de two horn an he dey do lek say he dey draw. So when he dey do dis he see den people den dey come yonder wid plenty cow. Wen den reach close um he tell den say, "Oona, come hep me; make we pull de king he cow fom dis hole." So den people begin fo go take de rope an wen den draw, de cow heen head come out na de hole. Spider mek lek he dun vex pon um. He say: "Yo dun cut de chief heen cow head. If oona no gie six cow I dey go tell de chief an oona go get big plabber." So den people gie um six cow, an he go. He dey laugh den people.'

"Devils are supposed to dwell under cotton-trees, in thick groves, at the sources of rivers, upon mountains. They are reverenced as presiding over all things. They may be increased and propitiated. Porroh devils are never to be seen except by some principal men in the society. Bundoo devils dance openly, publicly. On special occasions devils, corresponding somewhat to circus clowns, dance for the amusement of the people. This any intelligent, nimble native is permitted to do. Devil is not used in the sense of Satan. There is not one supreme power over all others, but some idea of rank may exist. Devils are, to some extent, believed in as sort of heathen guardian angels. Fire and war are supposed to result from a devil's wrath, to appease which sacrifices are offered. In case of war fighting follows the sacrifices. If victorious, the people beg pardon for the offense that brought on the war; if they are conquered, they beg the more. In case of war at Shaingay, Tasso would be the sacrificial site. There used to be a town, Kobotuma, near Bagru, that had such a strong devil as protector that when war came he placed a heavy bush before the town, and thus rendered it invisible. Mt. Kuno, by Bishop Mills christened Mt. Mary, is believed to be inhabited by all the dead of that portion of the country. One person only can go there, the priest of the mountain, who worships and entreats for the people. He takes with him white rice, a white fowl, oil, and a white country cloth. He remains a day or longer. Alphonso and Mr. Evans, when up there, heard of the priest being absent a month. The town on the mountain is invisible to the natural eye. There the dead carry on this life's occupations. In a spring at the foot of the mountain all kinds of fine fish are said to abound, and no one dares investigate. When people in the valley wail for the dead, voices from Mt. Kuno call out, 'Don't cry down there. He's up here.'

"Spirits are supposed to live the same as in this life. Class condition does not change; master remains master; slave remains slave. This implied belief in resurrection is not universal. A class, presumably a small class, claims that this life ends all. Spirits of the dead are not devils, but 'die pussons.' To the spirits of the old and influential worship is directed. Graves are dug shallow that the spirits of the interred may come forth. If one desires the grave deeper, another may ask, 'What has the dead done to you that you do not wish him to return?' Alphonso told of some people who claimed to see spirits come from the Cockboro River for his father at his death. They carried lanterns. Part of the number turned back, and as they did so called to the advancing ones to bring them some scent when they returned. All the dead from Shaingay are to go to that place on Cockboro River. An island used to travel back and forth from Cockboro River to Plantain, perhaps as a sort of portable bier. A few days ago an immense tree became uprooted and floated slowly past Shaingay. Its far-reaching branches above the water had the appearance of an island. We saw a boat passing at some distance from the tree, and were told that its occupants lowered the sail and passed softly, believing a devil to be traveling by. When a cotton-tree is cut down wine is poured on the roots so the spirits may not be offended.

This subject is a difficult one on which to obtain accurate information. Probably this typewriter could be worn to its last letter in recording a small portion of the uncanny and varying superstitions of this deluded race."

CHAPTER VII.

"THE OPEN DOOR.

"Across the valley which lies before my window, mounds of fresh earth speak of the presence of newly-planted batteries that stand as faithful watch-dogs at the harbor of Sierra Leone. Just round the hill the foundation for a powerful search-light is already laid, and even as I write, warships are passing with troops and supplies destined for a disturbed section on the Niger, while trained diplomats, representing the British and French, are met to-day in Paris to draw still more definitely the colonial lines on the face of this continent. Why is all this outlay of money, and what means this array of troops on a shore only narrowly fringed with civilization, if this point be not regarded as singularly strategic? With all the wealth of the British Empire there is no money to waste on useless fortresses, and as surely as this colony holds the key to military operations on this coast, it in turn offers an open door to Christian missions.

"Following the western shore for one thousand eight hundred miles north to the Strait of Gibraltar, a Christian missionary will find no hospitable land where the preaching of a simple, searching truth will be welcomed or tolerated as here in Sierra Leone. To the north and east are the fanatical lands of the Pope and false prophet. There is a population of 9,450,000 within French territory, with only two Protestant mission stations and three missionaries—one missionary to three million. While the whole heathen world presents a dearth of workers, this excessively needy field can hold the Pope-ridden government, by which it is ruled, largely responsible for holding back, by vexing conditions, the missionaries who would enter this Oriental empire. But our God is stronger than the nations, and so in this colony there is given to the church the opportunity of developing a missionary center from which this whole great country may be reached. If we were to have a Pentecost in Freetown to-day, the scene would not be unlike the one of long ago, since it is estimated that seventy different languages are spoken here. This means that to this colony and city come traders and travelers from remote nations. While Romanism may league with Mohammedanism and block the way for foreign missionaries, no human power can so control human speech as to stop the story of Jesus on the French frontier, when these wandering pagans have here been led to the feet of our Messiah. This opportunity ought to be a reason for thanksgiving, as well as the occasion for a determined effort to make the most of the opportunity which God has so unmistakably thrust within our hands, to teach and train the thousands of workers upon whom eventually the burden of evangelization must rest.

"But why not thrust that responsibility immediately upon native agencies, some may inquire? The answer is not farther away than a good map of this continent. The length and breadth of this great country is not well understood. By following the tenth parallel, north latitude, across this continent one would travel 4,430 miles, a distance nearly as great as from New York to Hawaii, or from Florida to Behring Strait. In this long journey there is not one Christian missionary. People grow eloquent and importunate over the demands of home missions, and granting that there is abundant work to do at home, one needs to lock the doors of every theological seminary, college, and public school, and to seal the lips of every minister or Christian teacher; one needs to banish every trained physician, to mine every wall that stands as a protection to the insane, the blind, deaf, dumb, poor, or criminal classes, and to annul every law that protects the Christian Sabbath or personal purity, in order that one may secure a condition at home like the actual condition that touches our borders this moment. No trace of these would one find in that weary walk across this continent. And yet in the great Sudan and its adjacent provinces there are one hundred million people—one hundred million people for whom Christ died and to whom they all are precious. Oh, servants of Christ, the load is too great to put on any native church, devoted though it may be. Pray the Father to thrust out immediately other laborers into the white wasting harvest.

"To this colony our church has unmistakably been led. Revivals have repeatedly revealed the stamp of God upon the work, and we find a large field open to us that is recognized as our peculiar territory by other Protestant bodies. Running eastward from Shaingay is a line of cities that demand immediate occupation. The one farthest interior is fourteen days' journey from the coast. Distance, it must be remembered, is only relative, and these cities occupy about the same relation to each other as Liverpool, New York, Omaha, and San Francisco. Beyond the first two, practically nothing has been attempted, so that pioneers are needed there to organize a campaign that shall include many hundreds of smaller villages. Passing to the northward from these cities are five others equally important, which connect advantageously with those stations already occupied by the Woman's Missionary Association. No more solemn obligation ever rested on any people than rests on us, as we now confront this field which waits for our sowing. Prayers have gone up to our Father to open the doors, and the doors are wide open. Better the prayer had never been offered than to refuse to enter now. An increased number of foreigners would afford an opportunity for the employment of ten times the present force of native agents. The native men who must bear a great deal of this burden are necessarily placed into active service long before they should be asked or expected to bear such responsibilities. The young men themselves need to be taught during their first years of service, and where distances are so great it is practically impossible to keep them in close connection with the schools already established. What the Master did for the twelve, others should do in each of these central cities. Paul must gather round him his Luke, Marcus, and Timothy. That being accomplished, the apostle will move on to regions more remote till all the land is gone over. All this the church intends exactly to fulfill, but it takes so long, and will take long, until the Great Commission is read with grammatical care—till the personal 'Go ye' is no longer broadened into 'Go church.' The responsibility is individual and direct.

"A peculiar condition exists here from the fact that on the bosom of this continent the descendants of Shem, Ham, and Japheth contend for empire, and make more complicated a task that is never easy. Who is sufficient for these things? Who should apply? Certainly not those who shrink from the stern duties at home and would seek a less exacting sphere; on the contrary, those demanded at home, as some may think because of special gifts, are the very men whom Africa calls to her rescue. If Ethiopia is saved, it will be by the best gifts that Christian nations can bestow upon her—the choice sons and daughters of their own lands.

"To those, I would appeal, who are debating the choice of a life service. Not that I would be careless of your ambitions, or by one word would induce you to enlist in a warfare unworthy your best efforts, but rather with a full appreciation of what your consecrated energies are worth, with an ever-widening sympathy for these millions, and with an ever-broadening conception of the fruits of missionary endeavor, and an ever-deepening joy in the service itself, I would have you give your life here. When your numbers are thought of, I could wish the return of Peter the Hermit that he might stir to the depths our dull spirits till again the crusades should be gathered, not, indeed, to carry votive offerings to the sepulcher of a dead Christ but to carry knowledge of that Christ resurrected to the sepulchers of those dead in trespasses and in sin. Nothing less than the preaching of a new crusade can settle the present problems of the foreign field—a crusade that shall enlist not a mission board, but the church; a crusade that shall draw from every Christian nation the choice workmen, with the funds necessary for their maintenance in the dark places of the earth; a crusade that floods the church with knowledge of actual heathenism, of deeds darker than the Saracens ever practiced at the Holy Sepulcher; a crusade of truth that shall declare with ceaseless energy that those *who are without God are without hope in the world.*

"The spirit of heroism is not dead in the breasts of the strong men and women of the church, neither is the spirit of philanthropy unknown to those whom God has chosen as stewards of large fortunes. Whose is the far-reaching voice that shall speak with such decision that the church will believe that this is the year for an immediate advance, the year to pay one hundred thousand dollars into the Lord's treasury for missions, the year to occupy ten great heathen centers in this important colony. Within a year a country has been opened on the Niger, one thousand miles in length by six hundred in breadth, equal to fourteen states like Ohio. There lies before me as I write a challenge from Bishop Tugwell, of the C. M. S., to the whole Christian world to occupy and make Jesus king over this newly-created empire. Shall this challenge be cravenly disregarded? Will the light of this century go out with that magnificent colony eagerly occupied by men engaged in the extension of trade while Christian men are too spiritless to hasten the extension of truth? It is not a man shapen in dreams that stands and utters in the night the cry for help, but the ringing cry of a man of flesh and blood in broad day. May our God command the forces that shall move obediently upon the great Sudan through this new broad highway.

"You men of the church who hold positions of influence as superintendents, trustees, class-leaders are responsible for your church, your Sabbath school, your Christian Endeavor Society. The thrifty church of the future without its missionary will be as anomalous as a church now without a Sabbath school or young people's society. What are you going to do for this hundred million of people, the brethren of the Lord and dear to him as your brother, your son, or your wife? This hundred million that live to the east and north of us would people the important State of Indiana fifty times, or the State of Nebraska one hundred times. Surely there is a duty here for business men. When the week closes and books are balanced, will you take a map of Africa, with statistics appended, and make it balance with the New Testament? By your study your heart will be enlisted to give or to go, as the Master directs. The joy of obedience will be your rich reward. Upon your head, at no distant day, will loving hands be laid as our returning Lord stands glorified on Mt. Olivet, and says to you who have shared devotedly in the rescue of these lost, loved races: 'Come, ye blessed of my Father, inherit the kingdom prepared for you from the foundation of the world.' Even so come quickly, Lord Jesus."—*Alfred T. Howard.*

CHAPTER VIII.

THE MASSACRE.

The preceding part of this work was planned before the recent burning of our mission property and the massacre of our devoted band of missionaries at Rotufunk and Taiama. The wilderness that had been glad for them, and the desert that had begun to blossom as the rose, during the latter part of April and the early part of May (1898), were visited by a heathen, infuriated mob, and seven American missionaries, several native missionaries, and several hundred converts were cruelly murdered, and over fifty thousand dollars worth of property was destroyed.

Just before the holidays a new force of laborers had reached the field, consisting of Rev. I. N. Cain and wife, Marietta Hatfield, M.D., Ella Schenck, and Arthur Ward, for Rotufunk, and Rev. L. O. Burtner and wife, for Shaingay.

The annual conference was held at Shaingay during the holidays. The new parties had settled down to the work; of the former force, Rev. J. R. King and wife had just returned home, followed by Prof. A. T. Howard and wife, and the Misses Cronise and Eaton (all needing rest and change of climate), when this appalling calamity swept over the mission like a hurricane.

There had been heard mutterings of discontent against the reforms and civilizing efforts of the British, but it was hoped no harm would come of

Mission House, Shaingay.

it, or that, at least, no one could be found who would harm these missionaries. But when the mob arose, excited to frenzy by their native orators, they sought to destroy every white person and every friend of the white man, so far as possible. It was the last struggle in Sierra Leone of Mohammedan blind zeal and heathen rage to stay the progress of Christian civilization.

At the advice of the British governor, the other American missionaries, Rev. L. O. Burtner and wife, Rev. F. S. Minshall and wife and babe, and Mr. Arthur Ward, wisely returned home to await the overthrow of the mob by British arms and the return of peace.

The following, from Rev. L. O. Burtner, is a very full account:

"SIERRA LEONE WARS.

"When homeward bound, in Liverpool and New York, our party was interviewed by various newspaper reporters. It is due to the party, the church, and the friends of the massacred to say that the newspapers too often report more than they have to report. Too much liberty is given to the imagination and too little attention to accuracy.

"*Causes of the Uprising.*—In my judgment no one thing can be assigned as the cause of the outbreak. About six or eight years ago the government began more fully to express its interest in the colony by undertaking to suppress the slave-trade carried on by and among the natives, the chiefs and big men among them profiting most by the traffic.

"Later an attempt was made to abolish cannibalism. A half dozen or more persons were tried, convicted, and hanged. Later still, two or three years ago, restrictions were put upon the Porroh, a secret society of the natives. All males are members, and occasionally one or more belong who do not wish to be regarded as or numbered among the heathen—persons who have been more or less taught in letters.

"The Porroh, as the natives regard it, is the law of the country, and when they would put Porroh (as they say) on any thing or person, no one dare interfere; if so, it is at the risk of his life. Porroh had been put on the palm kernels, and no one was allowed to gather them until the society saw fit to 'pull the Porroh.' Thus crop after crop would go to waste, and many poor people suffer in consequence of this waste. The government said this restriction of the Porroh must cease.

"About two years ago a protectorate was established, not including the original settlement of Sierra Leone and the Sherbro Island. The protectorate was divided into five districts, and a district commissioner, a white man, appointed to each. To these commissioners all matters of dispute and law were referred for final adjustment. A small hut tax was required by the government for its support and the maintenance of the protectorate and further development of the country—the making of roads, bridges, railroads, etc. The amount of the tax was five shillings, or one dollar and twenty-five cents, for a house of three rooms and under, and ten shillings, or two dollars and fifty cents, for a house of four or more rooms. The chiefs were to collect this tax and pay to the district commissioners, and they turn it over to the government.

"The people refused to pay. The Porroh had its meetings, killed its goats, and swore its 'one word' —that is, the first chief who collected and paid the hut tax would lose his head. The government said any one who refused to pay would be arrested and imprisoned, and some one, who would pay, would be appointed to take his place. The Temni tribe, located in the northern district, revolted, and made war on the government. They prepared strong and somewhat effective fortifications, and made a vigorous fight, so that it was necessary for the government to utilize all the troops immediately at hand in repulsing them. The other tribes, taking advantage of this engagement of the government with the Temnis, united their forces (a thing unknown in the history of the colony—hitherto they made war on each other), and made their raid against all foreigners, and Sierra Leoneans, black people, native born, and educated—in short, against all persons in sympathy with the civilization and Christianity which the government and church sought to establish and extend. Black Englishmen, as they sometimes call themselves in distinction from the heathen natives, shared the same fate as Europeans and Americans. Thus it was a war of heathenism against civilization and Christianity, a war of extermination of all who did not properly pronounce the 'shibboleth' of heathenism. And the causes leading up to it are (1) suppression of slavery, (2) suppression of cannibalism, (3) restrictions on the Porroh, (4) requiring the hut tax, the latter being the occasion for the outbreak.

"*Plan of Attack.*—Much skill and forethought seems to have been exercised in the plan of attack.

The uprising was almost simultaneous. Within two or three days the destruction of life and property respecting our missions and misssionaries was over, except in the case of Brother and Sister McGrew, which was five days later, May 8. It was rumored that the Mohammedans were in sympathy with the insurgents and assisted in formulating plans. I know not how true this is.

"*Implements of War.*—The 'war-boys' had clubs, swords, cutlasses (implements resembling our old-fashioned corn-choppers), and some guns and ammunition. During the past six or eight years the sale of firearms and ammunition to the natives had been prohibited by the government. It was supposed that they were without either. How and where they secured these is an unsettled question in the mind of the public.

"*Situation at Shaingay.*—I pass over many details. The first news of the war which made us quit our work and prepare for their coming was a letter from one G. M. Domingo, of Bompetook, which town is three hours' walk south of Shaingay, and also on the coast, to our chief, Thomas Neal Caulker. The chief promptly sent the letter to me at nine o'clock Saturday morning, April 30. The letter stated that the war-boys had taken Danville Mission, and that D. F. Wilberforce and wife were caught and tied, his mother shot, and sister and children killed, and the warriors were coming on Shaingay Mission. [It has since been learned that Mr. Wilberforce and family escaped, and are safe.] Brother Minshall and I began at once to fortify our mission house, and remained in it until Sunday night, May 1, about seven o'clock. We had determined not to leave the place, although we had only one revolver and seventy cartridges, and one old shotgun and a half-dozen loads of powder. The people, about five hundred, except forty-five, principally women and children yet with us, had been transferred to Plantain Island, six miles off the coast of Shaingay, during Saturday and Sunday. Among these were our mission boys and church members. Only three men were with us—Rev. J. A. Evans, A. T. Caulker, and C. A. Columbus.

"More carefully considering our environment, all the circumstances leading up to the situation, in a moment of awful suspense there came the conviction as if by inspiration from on high, *Anchor outside!* which meant to me secure refuge in the darkness of the night on the bosom of the sea. We started for Plantain Island. A few minutes rowing around the point brought us in full view of the burning of our mission properties at Mano, Kooloong, and Otterbein stations, just south of us. The warriors were then near Shaingay. But a little longer and we, too, should have fallen by their cruel hands. At midnight, May 1, we left Plantain Island, arrived at Kent at eight o'clock the evening of May 2, left there Tuesday morning at two o'clock, May 3, and arrived at Freetown Wednesday morning at six o'clock.

"On Monday, May 2, our people crossed Youra Bay from Plantain Island to Kent and other points nearer Freetown. The latest word I have from them is May 9, which is, 'We are all safe so far.' At Shaingay we had a large two-and-a-half-story mission house, stone structure and slate roof, a splendid stone church with slate roof, an excellent school building two-and-a-half-stories high, also of stone and an iron roof, a large two-story, seven-room house, lower story of stone, upper of frame structure and iron roof (this building was to be used for a dispensary and hospital), a large boys' home, a girls' home, two kitchens, two fowl houses, four out-buildings, one blacksmith shop, one boat-house large enough to house four boats (all these were frame buildings on stone foundations, and iron roofs), a nine-room native house with iron roof and veranda all around (this house was used as a parsonage), and two other excellent native buildings—sixteen buildings all in good state of preservation—now all destroyed.

"*Bonthe Station.*—Here our excellent nine-room mission house, rice-house, and large school-building, which we use for church purposes at present, are uninjured.

"*Avery Station.*—A large seven-room mission house, stone walls and iron roof, a splendid church and school-room, frame structure and iron roof, and an excellent sawmill, all said to be burned.

"Brother J. E. Hughes, one of our itinerants, and his wife and daughter were reported slain. C. A. Remmie, the other itinerant, being very sick, went to Bonthe the week before for treatment. His sister, Sarah Curtis, of Shaingay, was with him, so they escaped; no tidings from his wife and children with her at Avery were received.

"*Other Stations.*—Konkonany, Mattro, Jehovah, Mandoh, Otterbein, Kooloong, and Mano were reported burned.

"*Situation at Rotufunk.*—Of this I speak

with bated breath. Of the six missionaries there, five were killed—Rev. I. N. Cain and wife, Dr. Mary Archer, Dr. Marietta Hatfield, and Miss Ella Schenck. Doctor Hatfield was very ill. Mr. A. A. Ward had gone to Freetown on business a few days before, and thus escaped.

"Sunday and Monday nights, May 1 and 2, the five left the mission premises and slept in the bush, returning each morning to the mission house. Tuesday morning, about nine o'clock, the warriors entered the town. The missionaries again fled to the bush, but were soon stopped by the warriors, who had surrounded the town and anticipated the direction in which the missionaries would flee. They had gone about two hundred yards when brought back in front of the mission and killed. About ten o'clock on the morning of May 3 these missionaries finished the work our Lord gave them to do. Rev. L. A. McGrew and wife, of Taimai, also were slain, on May 8.

"'Why do the heathen rage, and the people imagine a vain thing? The kings of the earth set themselves, and the rulers take counsel together, against the Lord, and against his anointed, saying, Let us break their bands asunder, and cast away their cords from us.' 'And this is life eternal, that they might know thee the only true God, and Jesus Christ, whom thou hast sent.'

"There is a total loss of property here by fire. All the houses were frame buildings, with iron roofing, except the boys' home. Mission house, school-building, church, girls' home, boys' home, dispensary, industrial building, rice-house, and boat-house, all said to be totally destroyed.

"*What of the Future.*—Do we love God? All things work together for good to them that love God. Thrice Christ required Peter to answer this question. Let each member of the church answer it for himself.

"*Good to them that love God!* All who truly love will enlarge their contributions and consecration. God can and will make the wrath of men to praise him. Christ tested the rich young ruler by commands and promises. He went away from Christ and treasures in heaven. God is testing the faith and obedience of the church to-day. Let us stand the test, and in this the beginning of the second year of our missionary quadrennium and in this time of deepest sorrow, show our faith by our works. Give not only tithes, but large free-will offerings. Mother England will do her part, and God is the giver of every good and perfect gift, and never fails his children."

Prof. A. W. Drury, of the import of this great sacrifice, says:

"In some respects the most overwhelming of all missionary reverses occurred in connection with the Indian mutiny of 1857, when Mohammedanism and Brahmanism, supported by the darkest passions and superstitions of the native people, sought to overthrow British rule in India, and to extirpate everything foreign, Christianity, of course, included. In large cities and populous provinces fire, rapine, lust, and murder well nigh accomplished their satanic purposes. Thousands of foreigners were slain; thousands were subjected to revolting cruelties. The British army, under the Christian soldier, General Havelock, and other intrepid leaders, never fought against greater odds or administered a more crushing defeat. In the disturbed districts missions were everywhere destroyed, a number of missionaries being slain. The most noted example of martyrdom was that of eight missionaries of the American Presbyterian Church, Mr. and Mrs. Freeman, Mr. and Mrs. Johnson, Mr. and Mrs. McMullin, and Mr. and Mrs. Campbell with their two children, who with many others sought refuge in boats on the Ganges, and were afterward captured and taken to the parade grounds of Cawnpore and ruthlessly shot. The noble character and bearing of the missionaries gave luster to the Christian name. As a result of the great crisis conditions favorable to the evangelizing of India were permanently established, a greater missionary interest excited, and the pace of mission work quickened. To-day we are beginning to hear of a national church of India. The possibility of speedy changes in favor of human weal after threatened overthrow is emphasized by the fact that the year following the mutiny, the year 1858, was more widely signalized by the opening up of new fields for the gospel than any previous year in Christian history.

"Madagascar has been spoken of as a field specially consecrated by the blood of martyrs, but the martyrs have been from the ranks of native Christians. In no other country have native Christians been more courageous in the face of danger or more faithful when missionaries have withdrawn or been expelled.

"The fall of our missionaries will not be to us in vain if it lays in the dust the maxims of selfishness, and enthrones a higher manhood in human hearts. We may adopt the language of Bishop Fowler with reference to the noble contagion that comes from the labors and sacrifices of missionaries. He says: 'It is worth more than all it costs to have the home church feel a kinship to these heroic souls. When a country cannot produce among her own sons men willing to die for their liberties, but must do her fighting by mercenaries, then that country has lost her liberties, and has nothing left worth dying for. When a church reaches a state where she cannot furnish missionaries and keep in sympathy with her missionaries she has reached a point where she has nothing worth propagating. It is the spirit of heroism and sacrifice that insures spiritual triumph. . . . No church can long remain a conquering force which has not the missionary spirit, and does not understand the word of Jesus, "As the Father hath sent me, even so send I you." There run through the ages great lines of spiritual power that lift and mold mankind. . . . These lines can be seized only by the writhing hands of sacrifice. . . . It is not all loss to sacrifice for God; often all else is loss.' Should the world be wholly evangelized and no place left for literal martyrdom, it would yet require pierced hands to lift it to higher planes of character and action. For the individual soul, here and hereafter, redemption means not merely the price paid by Christ, but also the spirit of sacrifice enthroned in human hearts."

I have elsewhere said and now repeat that the law of sacrifice is the first law of the kingdom of God. The life of the Master illustrated this fact, for even "the Son of man came not to be ministered unto, but to minister, and to give his life a ransom for many." From the beginning obedience to this law has been the condition of human progress. The mother gives her life for her child, the patriot dies for his country, and the *missionary* dies for his King.

When Brother Cain refused to fire on the black mob ready to slay the little party of whites, I have no doubt he consulted his noble comrades, and they said, "Let us lay down our lives for Africa, even as our Saviour did for us." And they were at once enrolled in the great army of martyrs, who counted not their own lives dear unto themselves. The redemption of Africa goes forward by such service. The graves of Christian missionaries and explorers are the stepping-stones across the Dark Continent. It has pleased God to give our church the honor of furnishing a glorious band, who by this high offering of sacrificial service has done so much to redeem Africa.

Other churches and other fathers and mothers have made similar offerings of their most precious sons and daughters. They are an offering unto the Lord of hosts, and are enrolled in his book. The missionary, Krapf, dying in the Galla country, bequeathed "to every missionary coming to east Africa" the "idea of a chain of missions" across the entire Dark Continent. He said, "The first resident of the new mission ground is a dead person of the missionary circle; our God bids us first build a cemetery before we build a church or dwelling-house, showing us by this lesson that the resurrection of east Africa must be affected by our own destruction."

As the sacrifices which the earth has cost make it more deeply interesting and precious to heaven, so these sacrifices for Africa will make it dearer and nearer to the hearts of all our people. Such royal investments in that land will call forth still more; for as Missionary Cox said, "Though a thousand fall let not Africa be given up."

While we to-day sorrow with the bereaved homes, through our tears we look up to our Great Commander and to the group of martyrs ascended to his presence, and greet him and them, saying, "*We offer a larger number of equally heroic souls for Africa. Command! it is our joy to obey.*"

This statement represents the sentiments of the officers and members of both of our missionary societies, and of our whole church.

Mrs. L. K. Miller, editor of the *Woman's Evangel,* expresses the sorrow and hope of all, in the following beautiful poem, entitled:

"OUR MARTYRED FRIENDS.

" For this sweet task, O blessed Christ, inspire
  My thought! As thee in dark Gethsemane
  The angel soothed, and, with his holy touch,
  New strength bestowed to fit thee for thy cru-
  Cial hour, so strength divine impart to-day.

" As, years agone, the toys, the shoes, the hat
  Of my own darling boy I held and said,
  'These, *these* are all that's left,' while burning tears
  Like rain fell o'er them, so to-day I hold
  The things that once were theirs — these letters sweet
  That came oft from afar, and made this old
  EVANGEL ever new — gave it new wings
  To fly the nations o'er, bearing sweet words
  Of hope and joy, of wide, deep plans achieved,

Of plans that reach out into coming years;
I clasp these letters tight and cry in grief
Too deep for sounding line to mete, 'Alas!
These, *these* are all that's left!'

       "Be still, sad heart!
Full well thou know'st thy darling boy hath blest
Each year, each day that stretcheth through the year,
And made thee strong to bear, to do for love's
Own sake. These, whom with love's eternal cord
So tight you hold, are only gone away —
Like Moses, hid by God among the clouds
On Nebo's heights, in fiery chariot snatched
Away from earth — so like the holy Christ,
Sore bruised, and pierced, and mocked, and basely slain.

"Oh, think! thou canst not weigh their holy joy
To-day, as by the Crucified they stand
And show their wounds for love of him received —
For love of *his lost sheep* he came to save —
Poor Afric's sons. O heart of pity, break
Anew o'er these who blindly slew their Lord!
'Ye did it unto me.' *They knew it not.*
O heart of pity, break anew, and plead
For these lost souls who dared to slay Christ's own!
Thus, thus we deem our martyred ones to-day
Stand near their Lord presenting oft their wounds.
They live, they live! who dares to think them dead?
As years and ages come and go, they'll live
To plead for that black land drenched with their blood,
The land for which they died.

"We see them, aye, we hear each voice to-day,
As, bending just above, scarce out of sight,
They cast their martyr crowns before the Lamb
Who erst was slain;
With broken hearts we clasp their spirit hands,
And join with them before the throne to plead

For Afric's poor black sheep — the Shepherd's own
Redeemed, yet age on age in heathen night
Enchained by Satan's hellish power — his slaves!

"We plight anew our lives to earnest toil;
This martyred host forever live! and live
In us; and in these pages where their lives
Were wont to shine — here they must live and breathe,
And bless our toil, and make us brave to win
The lost world back to Christ. *It must not be*
That these, our well belov'd, have died in vain."

PART II

MEMOIRS OF OUR HEROIC DEAD IN SIERRA LEONE, WEST AFRICA

REV. I. N. CAIN.

PART II

MEMOIRS OF OUR HEROIC DEAD IN SIERRA LEONE, WEST AFRICA

Massacred at Rotufunk, West Africa, May 3, 1898.

1. Rev. I. N. Cain, A.B.
2. Mrs. I. N. Cain, A.B.
3. Miss Mary C. Archer, M.D.
4. Miss Marietta Hatfield, M.D.
5. Miss Ella Schenck.

Massacred at Taiama, West Africa, May 9, 1898.

6. Rev. Lowry A. McGrew.
7. Mrs. Clara B. McGrew.

Died of fever at Rotufunk, West Africa.

8. Rev. Richard N. West.
9. Miss Frances Williams.
10. Miss Elma Bittle.

Died of apoplexy at Freetown, West Africa.

11. Rev. Joseph Gomer.

"These all died in faith, not having received the promises, but having seen them and greeted them from afar, and having confessed that they were strangers and pilgrims on the earth. For they that say such things make it manifest that they are seeking after a country of their own. And if indeed they had been mindful of that country from which they went out, they would have had opportunity to return. But now they desire a better country, that is, a heavenly: wherefore God is not ashamed of them, to be called their God: for he hath prepared for them a city" (Heb. 11: 13-16, R. V.).

The following papers are of different lengths, not because of any difference in the merits of their subjects, but because of our inability to get all the facts desired of some of them.

They are not written for the eye of the literary critic, but they are flowers of affection from the gardens of the hearts of loving friends, laid tenderly upon our martyrs' graves.

ISAAC NEWTON CAIN

was born near Cainsville, Missouri, August 28, 1864, and was the sixth in a family of ten children. When the lad was eight years old his mother died, and four years later his father also died. Left early to care for himself, he developed a self-reliance of rare value. In 1881 he was converted, while living near West Union, Iowa. In 1885 he entered Western College, and began to prepare for his life work. By teaching part of the time, and taking a pastoral charge at another time, he earned the money that enabled him to complete a college course, graduating in 1892, a bachelor of science. In August following he was married to a classmate, Miss Mary E. Mutch, and soon after sailed for Rotufunk, West Africa, under the employment of the Woman's Missionary Board.

Mr. Cain and his wife served in the mission field for three and one-half years, then returned for rest and change of climate. Both he and his wife returned to their *alma mater* during the year of rest and completed the classical course of study.

In the autumn of 1897, they both went back to Rotufunk, Africa, for a five years' term, but death claimed them on the third day of May following. They were massacred by those they sought to bless and save.

Mr. Cain was tall and graceful in person, with pleasant face and easy presence. He was noted as a diligent student, and his goodness of heart made him a favorite among all his acquaintances.

His practical turn of mind led him to experiment in making bricks, and building a chapel at Rokon out of the same. This element of his nature was of great value to the field he served.

He was a good teacher and preacher, and above all a courteous, conscientious, cultured Christian gentleman, of a type rarely found.

Personal Impressions of Rev. I. N. Cain.

By Alfred T. Howard, A.M.

Not only beauty is in the rose, though the rose is beautiful. Not only strength is in the hills, though the hills are strong. Not all virtues are equally shown in the characters of men, however much those characters command our admiration. As this testimony is given to the personal qualities of a fallen comrade I would not be understood to mean that these qualities by which I have been most deeply impressed were the only virtues that graced his splendid character. Among men whom I have known he was the most unselfish. That unselfishness was shown by his pledge to foreign service when proposals that were almost entreaties were being made to keep him at home. But he was a man with a conscience that ruled him thoroughly, so when personal ambition and inclination were weighed against the needs of heathen men self lost, God and the heathen won.

Once on the foreign field he was in no haste to assume control, but took a subordinate position given him in the school, filling it as willingly as though it had been a professorship in his own Western College. Outside of school his was the careful, ceaseless task of overlooking a whole great company of boys and teaching them habits of industry, punctuality, thoroughness, and thrift by personal association and example. Under his direction the boys began to make brick, which may mean little enough to comfortable people in America, but in a country where houses of clay have for centuries been the homes of the people, and where white ants mischievously destroy any structure of wood, the man who instructs the people to build permanent homes will check the nomadic character of Mendi and Temni men, and make of these wanderers, citizens. The beginning of this task was not easy.

I always admired Mr. Cain for the approval he gave his predecessor in the superintendency. After my own experiences in the tropics, the land of everlasting August, I incline to the belief that criticism is indigenous to the soil. But few methods of missionary operation have been tried sufficiently long to secure for them universal and absolute confidence. It is so easy then in that provokingly hot country to blame one's associates for what Satan himself is responsible. Mr. Cain always discovered the best qualities in his associates. When he took up the superintendency of the Bompeh mission, there was no minimizing the work of his predecessor to make his own labor appear to better advantage. I remember sitting with him in a native house at Mocourri in the Mendi country, and while speaking of the early work and workers, he said, "I tell you I liked Brother West. He was a great missionary." His appreciation of Brother West's years of faithful toil always won for him the confidence of his associates in his own administration. Without any change of policy he took up the work and sought earnestly to extend it into the interior, which had always engaged his keenest interest.

Personal conviction is, and must continue to be, of great weight in mission work. Certainly this has its benefits, but there is an embarrassment that sometimes comes to a superintendent who must adjust these personal convictions to the most urgent needs of the field. Mr. Cain would change his own plans again and again that every missionary might be in a place, so far as possible, congenial to his inclinations. I never could tell what he did not like to do. He made no complaints.

A second characteristic was his enthusiasm. I

have never seen Western College, and yet I think there is hardly an old student of that institution, or a nook or corner in that building, with which I am unacquainted. He would talk of Western College by the hour, exhibiting a loyalty that could not fail to win admiration. If that college has many alumni like him, its perpetuity is altogether secure. I doubt whether any financial agent in the co-operating conferences could do more earnest talking than this man did out of downright heart love, six thousand miles away. His interest in the great country that lay to the east of Sierra Leone was only equaled by the belief that God had called our church to that special work, and that we were able to go up and take the land. Wherever his testimony to the cause of missions was given there was in it the ring of confidence, and in his company confidence was contagious. This confidence in men won for him the love of the people who knew him. Between him and his boatmen or hammock men there was an attachment not usually observed between a white man and a native laborer. I have traveled with him in the country and heard him and his favorite hammock boys, "Boat," "Roggy," and "Two Copper," laughing together as they ran along, as merrily as though they were all companions with equal gifts. It must still be proved that these lowly friends of his knew of the plot to take his life in time to rescue him and his companion martyrs. Here and there among the disciples there may be a Judas, but compared with the faithful the unfaithful are few. Human hearts cannot be trusted as our brother trusted them, without giving a generous response. Let him who places no reliance on men of another race go out and demonstrate the truth, or folly, of his belief. Mr. Cain believed every man worthy of confidence till he found that man untrue. Having loved his own, he loved them unto the last.

To an English officer who was stopping with him for a few days, not long before the rebellion, he said, "Do, captain, remember our people. They may do wrong, but they are ignorant." Those who knew him best were not surprised to learn his last words. When that infuriated mass of men gathered around him, and he held in his hand a revolver that could have killed a number of his enemies, he threw the weapon away, and said, "I will not have any man's blood on my hands." That statement will do to go down on the records with the words of our Lord: "Father, forgive them; for they know not what they do"; and of Stephen: "Lord, lay not this sin to their charge." Faithful watchman, like Ezekiel, he lifted his voice to warn the people of their danger during his life, and in death no blood of his fellow-men stained his garments. A foreign land, a hateful climate, raging, ignorant enemies were exchanged in one eventful morning as he walked out, not knowing whither he went, for the long homeland, the breezes that spring from the healthful shade of the tree of life, the association of his kindred, the redeemed—wondrous transition! Earth, enemies; heaven, Jesus.

Long before we quit these mortal shores he has joined that innumerable company which no man can number, of all nations, and kindred, and people, and tongues, standing before the throne, and before the Lamb, clothed with white robes, and palms in their hands—"these are they which came out of great tribulation, and have washed their robes, and made them white in the blood of the Lamb. . . . They shall hunger no more, neither thirst any more; neither shall the sun light on them, nor any heat. For the Lamb which is in the midst of the throne shall feed them, and shall lead them unto living fountains of waters: and God shall wipe away all tears from their eyes."

Mary Elizabeth Mutch Cain.
BY UNCLE STEWART FORBES.

Mary E. Mutch was born October 28, 1860, in Hillsboro, Wisconsin. She was the second in a family of ten children—five sons and five daughters. Her father was a Scotchman of sterling worth, who served his adopted country in the Forty-ninth Wisconsin Infantry during the Civil War, and died after the close of the War from the effects of camp life.

Her mother's maiden name was Sarah Keller, a descendant of the early Dutch settlers on the Mohawk.

From both parents the subject of this sketch inherited noble moral and intellectual qualities, and was early inspired with high ideals of life.

Mrs. Cain, from her tender childhood, was noted for her kind and gentle disposition, to use her mother's words. She loved religion from a child, and early became an object of affectionate regard among her large circle of relatives and associates. Of a studious nature, she early manifested an aptitude for acquiring useful knowledge, and a laudable ambition to attain to the qualifications

MRS. MARY M. CAIN.

necessary to fit her for a school-teacher. With this aim in view, she proved an apt and progressive pupil, and for her gentle and unassuming deportment she was held in high esteem by teachers and schoolmates. When she was about seventeen, she taught her first school for about two years, as nearly as we can remember. Previous to commencing life as a teacher, Mrs. Cain made a public profession of her faith in Jesus Christ, as offered in the gospel, by becoming a member of the United Brethren Church, on Millard's Prairie, and was baptized by immersion. That she has ever since adorned her profession with a becoming grace, her beautiful life, so full of goodness, the outflow of a meek and gentle spirit, the excellent example she set for her associates in the different places where her duties as a teacher led her, are a bright and living testimony of the Christian worth of one who being dead, yet speaketh. Her motto was onward and upward. Teaching and attending the seminary by turns, she used her money to advance her knowledge in the higher branches. Her certificates received during the ten years she taught school show a steady advance from third to first grade, and prove her industry and high aims to attain success. As a teacher, and in the manner of conducting a school, Mrs. Cain was progressive as in everything else. Commencing to teach so young, it was feared by some that her gentle nature and reluctance to resort to severe measures to control refractory pupils, would mar her success in the line of order, but her record as a first-class teacher in the ten years she followed that important calling, and in different parts of the State, proved her capability in every respect, and her courteous and ladylike mien and carriage gained her hosts of friends wherever she went.

Mrs. Cain was ever a loving and dutiful daughter and affectionate sister. Her eldest brother, a fine young man of twenty-two, had a large share of his sister's love, which he appreciated with a brother's affectionate return. His sad, untimely death from an accident, while braking on the railroad, shed a gloom over the family.

The father's deep anguish; the heart-stricken cry
  Of sisters and brothers for him they loved dear;
How the grief-stricken mother, by faith looked on high,
  And a home for her darling she saw through her tears.

In less than three years the father, after a lingering illness, followed the son, in his fifty-first year. Of a large family, and her father often ailing since the War, Mrs. Cain showed her deep affection by affording the means out of her school earnings, to enable her two younger sisters to attend the seminary and high school at Elroy until they were qualified to teach. Although Mrs. Cain when a girl loved to mingle among her large circle of kindred associates and friends for pleasant pastime on occasions, yet she was of too serious a turn of mind to be a party in anything that appeared to her to be frivolous, or out of place for her high ideal of Christian life. She shunned dancing parties entirely, even the little home affairs in the neighborhood; otherwise she enjoyed a social gathering among her relatives and friends very much, and contributed to the enjoyment of the hour by her musical talents and sweet, mellow voice in singing, and otherwise making the time pleasant to old and young, alike; and those social home gatherings of kindred ties and friends are pleasant memories of bygone years.

Having in her early girlhood chosen that good part which the other Mary chose, it seemed to be the desire of her heart, and the aim of her well-trained mind, to abstain from every appearance of evil. She ever strove to attain to the highest ideal of a pure, true woman in Christ. And so conscientious was she in the duties pertaining to practical life that the Master's injunction, "Let your light so shine before men, that they may see your good works, and gorify your Father which is in heaven," appeared to be her sincere desire to follow in all that she did or said. The following pen picture of true womanhood, written of a dear relative* of Mrs. Cain's, is, in our mind, descriptive of herself:

> "God's lyric on earth is a woman,
>   With a loving heart, tender and true;
> Her mind, like a bright summer day-dawn,
>   All balmy with fragrance and dew;
> As mother or daughter, as sister or wife,
> A heaven-dropped melody, cheering all life.
>
> "A mixture of Mary and Martha,
>   Of Dorcas, of Hannah and Ruth,
> Of Eve, and the daughter of Jephthah,
>   With Esther a heroine in truth —
> A rare composition of everything nice,
> And far above pearls or rubies her price."

After a period of ten years of school-teaching except the times she attended the higher schools,

---

* An aunt of Mrs. Cain, and precious wife of the writer, among Mrs. Cain's last letters home, and one of sweet condolence to us.

Mrs. Cain, in 1888, entered Western College, Iowa. It was there she first met Mr. Cain, and where was formed those tender sentiments of mutual affection and true love which resulted in their union for life. They both graduated in 1892, in the scientific course, and their marriage was celebrated at the home of the bride's mother in the month of August following, in the presence of a large gathering of kindred and friends, Rev. D. C. Talbot officiating. They sailed for Sierra Leone in October following, and returned to their mother's home, in Elroy, in June, 1896, where, aside from another term at Western College, to complete the classical course, they made their home till they left for Sierra Leone the second time. During their stay with their mother here, their wide, warm-hearted, kind, and courteous bearing was highly appreciated among their large circle of relatives and friends in Elroy and vicinity.

They made many new acquaintances, who were glad of the same, and shed sunshine and pleasure wherever they came.

The different churches were opened invitingly for them to hold missionary services, or to lecture. Mr. Cain preached several times, by special request, on the absence of pastors. Both took a liberal interest in Sunday-school work and in other societies of the church, ever manifesting their heartfelt desire to be about the Master's business. They were always welcome guests at the homes of their relatives and friends, who felt their presence to be a benison of glad, social enjoyment.

The writer of these pages, and others, will not soon forget the picnic gathering at the pleasant home and shady lawn of our son-in-law and daughter, near the old United Brethren Church, on Millard's Prairie. The party was gotten up as a testimony of kindred and friendly esteem for Mr. and Mrs. Cain, about to depart on their far-away journey. It was a day of pleasant associations, not unmixed with regrets at the thoughts of parting with them so soon. But little did we reckon of the dark cloud looming in the far tropical sky, or that the two precious forms who stood together on that day by the organ and joined their well-trained voices in sacred song, would ever become the victims of savage cruelty. In our simple minds we had trusted that the British government, appreciating (as we learned) the services of the United Brethren missions within their territory, would protect the mission homes and vicinity from lawless savages. We were told by Mr. Cain that the governor of Sierra Leone, at an assembly in which he was present, paid a high tribute in his speech to the missions and their good work in the territory.

Mr. and Mrs. Cain's departure for their mission was accompanied by the prayers and best wishes of all with whom they associated here, who knew and appreciated their sterling worth. And the tidings of their ruthless slaughter, with that of their associates in the good work, was a terrible shock to their loved ones, and to the whole community.

A brief sketch in reference to Mrs. Cain's brothers and sisters will close our work on these pages.

Out of a family of ten children, Mrs. Mutch has

now six left, three sons and three daughters; the daughters are all married. Ida, the oldest, and Nellie, the next, are married to brothers of the name of Main, and live in Barron County; the youngest, Nancy, to Charles Miller. They own and occupy the old homestead on Millard's Prairie. The sons are unmarried. The eldest, Charles, is in the laundry business at Viroqua. John's occupation is painting and calcimining. His home is with his mother in Elroy. James, the youngest, is attending the University, at Madison. A niece of Mr. Cain's, Maud, whom he and Mrs. Cain adopted, and consigned to their mother's care on returning to Africa, is now one of Mrs. Mutch's family, and goes to school.

Previous to disposing of her farm to her son-in-law, Mrs. Mutch purchased a house and lot in Elroy, and took up her residence here five years ago. Memorial services for Mr. and Mrs. Cain were held in the Methodist Episcopal Church, of which Mrs. Mutch is now a member, Rev. Mr. Gordon, pastor. Two lifelike, enlarged cabinet pictures of Mr. and Mrs. Cain stood in brackets on either side in front of the rostrum, bringing tearfully tender memories of the dear ones gone, to the large audience of Mrs. Mutch and family, sympathizing kindred, neighbors, and friends.

Mary C. Archer.
BY REV. BYRON J. CLARK.

Mary C. Archer was born in Madison County, Iowa, July 28, 1864, and died at Rotufunk, Africa, May 3, 1898, being thirty-three years, ten months, and twenty-six days old at the time of her tragic

Miss MARY C. ARCHER, M.D.

death. She was the oldest daughter of a family of six children. At eleven years of age her mother died, leaving Mary with special burdens for one of her age; the father kept the family together, and at the age of seventeen, Mary entered Callanan College, Des Moines, Iowa, where she spent three years. She had the advantage of a good country school in childhood, where she was well prepared for her college life. Like many young people who most appreciate a good education, she had to make her own way through school, providing the means of an education with her own hands; this she accomplished by occasionally teaching a term of school, and in other ways.

One year was spent in Western College, Toledo, Iowa, when she entered King Electric Medical College, Des Moines, Iowa, from which she graduated in 1888, and for six years she practiced medicine in her home city, meeting with eminent success. She was converted at the age of fourteen, and joined the United Brethren Church, and was an honored member until her martyrdom for the cause she loved. While living in Des Moines she most actively engaged in the work of the church, serving as Sunday-school superintendent, president of the Endeavor Society, an earnest worker in the Woman's Missionary Society, and during all this time teaching a class in the Sunday school. She is loved and most tenderly remembered by all who knew her, as a model of Christian example and faithfulness. The spirit of her life still lives in the work of the local church where she belonged. Oh, how we miss her, but how honored we feel to have on our church roll the name of one now in heaven, wearing a martyr's crown.

Doctor Archer was especially gifted as a writer and preacher, presenting a smooth, elegant, and magnetic style of arrangement in the matter of her composition. She would arrest the attention of the most careless listener, as well as interest the most profound thinker. How feelingly she could speak of her desires for the salvation of the lost; how fervent she would become in her appeals to the sinner and in her remonstrances to the faithless, half-hearted Christian; yet through it all she manifested such a sweet and tender sympathy as to touch and arouse the most cold and hardened heart, and bring about the best results in Christian evangelization.

It was in the summer of 1895, at a ministerial institute, at Cambridge, Iowa, when, in connection with the institute, the Woman's Missionary Association held a session, that she spoke of her acceptance of the call to the African field. How seriously she spoke of her call, and her longings to present Christ to the souls of that darkened land. And, in the fall of the same year she was ordained by Bishop J. S. Mills, at an annual conference held at Corning, Iowa, and immediately sailed for her chosen field. No more successful missionary ever entered Africa than our own beloved Sister Archer; she became an almost indispensable factor in the mission work at Rotufunk, caring for the other missionaries in their sickness; cheering them in their discouragements, by the sweet sunshine of her life; serving the mission as both their physician and pastor, her life was indeed a holy benediction to all. And then when the black faces of the natives, carrying with them some of

Miss Marietta Hatfield, M.D.

the most loathsome diseases, appeared at her office for treatment, while bathing their sores, or administering remedies, she never failed to present Christ to them. She was thoroughly in love with her work, and all felt it who knew her. She was cruelly murdered by those she sought to save, and for whom she had sacrificed home and strong attachments in the homeland. But how like her Saviour; he left his home in the sky, and came to earth to save mankind. How cruelly they treated him—crucified him among the thieves and robbers. Slain by those he had come to save! May the death of our beloved missionaries aid in the redemption of Africa. How costly is the field, and how precious the cause. Let us keep burning the light so nobly lighted by our martyred missionaries.

Doctor Archer's work in Africa, as pastor at Rotufunk, and at the same time medical missionary for the station, was one of great zeal and faithfulness in loving service for her Master. No diseased native was too loathsome, no mud hut was too humble to prevent her ministrations of mercy. Loved by co-laborers and natives alike, her most promising, youthful life was joyfully placed upon the high altar of sacrifice, an offering acceptable unto God.

MARIETTA HATFIELD.
BY REV. Z. T. HATFIELD.

Marietta Hatfield was born at Ludlow (now Potsdam), Miami County, Ohio, October 11, 1851, and was therefore in her forty-seventh year at the time of her tragic death. She was the third of a family of thirteen, eight of whom survived infancy and reached manhood and womanhood. Six of these, the writer, of Decatur, Illinois; M. F. Hatfield, of Terre Haute, Indiana; Oscar Hatfield, of Center, Ohio; Mrs. Clara Britton, of Potsdam, Ohio; Miss Mina Hatfield, of West Milton, Ohio; and Mrs. Emma Gregory, of Kansas City, Kansas, with an invalid mother, survive her.

She lived with her parents in the village of her birth until about sixteen years old, and attended the village school, the only educational advantage ever enjoyed, prior to attending the Woman's Medical College, of Cincinnati, Ohio, where she fitted herself for the mission field, save, perhaps, a term or two at a school under the supervision of the New Lights, at Merom, a small town on the Wabash River, in the western part of Sullivan County, Indiana. When about sixteen she began teaching, which profession she followed, more or less continuously, for a period of twenty years or more. She was remarkably successful and was never necessarily without employment in her calling. Her services were eagerly sought wherever she was known. In 1878 she went to Illinois and made her home with the writer, near Downs, McLean County, engaging in her much-loved work of teaching. A year was very pleasantly spent here, making many friends, who proved of much value when a few years later she returned to Illinois. Returning to Ohio, she, with two brothers and two sisters, some time afterward removed to Plainsfield, Indiana, fourteen miles southwest of Indianapolis, on the Illinois and St. Louis Railroad. After a residence of several months at the above-named place, she again went to Illinois, where her reputation as a teacher, made at her first coming, enabled her readily to find employment. Two or three years concluded her residence in that State, when a second time she removed to Potsdam, Ohio, taking with her a sister, Mina, and her invalid mother.

It was while living here, doubtless, that the purpose of becoming a missionary fully matured in her mind, and actual preparations for its consummation began. Having determined upon the medical branch of mission work, the first thing to be done was to acquire the necessary qualifications. This she set about at once. The term of school in which she was then employed expired about March 6, and on March 12, 1889, she matriculated at the above-named medical college, less than a week after the close of her school. Two years of hard work followed. Impelled by an intense longing for active service in the field of her choice, she would not lose even the vacation, but while other students returned home for rest and recuperation, she remained in the city pursuing her studies privately, availing herself of all the hospital advantages possible. When her class graduated she declined to do so, not, as a member of her class informed me, because she was any the less proficient or in any way less competent than the others for the duties of a physician, but because she desired the best qualifications possible to her time and means. Accordingly, she entered college for another term, graduating March 4, 1891.

Prior to this event she had applied to the Woman's Board of Missions of the Church of the

United Brethren in Christ, of which church she was a member, for work in Africa. The happiest day of her life was when the news reached her that she was accepted. She was consecrated to the work to which she gave her life the evening of May 22, in the United Brethren Church, at Decatur, Illinois, about ten weeks after her graduation.

The time intervening between this and her departure was occupied in preparation, very little being spent in visiting among her relatives. She sailed from New York for Liverpool in the *City of Chicago*, September 23, 1891, in company with the Misses Schenck and Bittle, the latter surviving the change of climate but eight months, the former becoming a fellow martyr. At Liverpool the company embarked on the *Angolia*, a British liner, about October 10, and landed at Freetown the twenty-ninth of the same month. In a few more days she was established in her quarters at Rotufunk, the first one that her church had recognized as exclusively a medical missionary. Her work was arduous. In consequence of the policy of gratuitous service her patients soon numbered four score or more per day.

The duties became onerous, and she sought a change of policy, that of requiring a compensation which to the patients would seem an equivalent for what they received. This proved a benefit in many ways. First, it reduced the number of patients and relieved her somewhat from over-taxation; yet with this reduction, in ten months she treated sixteen hundred patients. This, too, was accomplished with an expenditure of a little less than thirty dollars above receipts, a very great step

toward making this department self-supporting—
a point toward which she bent all her energies, and
which, she frequently said, must obtain. The benefit to the natives themselves was very great. It gave
them more faith in the remedies and a much
greater regard for the doctor. Notwithstanding
the hard work, the inconveniences arising from in-
adequate equipment, and the lack of counsel, she
loved her work. She loved it because it was the
Master's work. She worked and suffered in his
name.

Three years and more thus passed away when
the decision of the council of missionaries was
to send Mrs. West and the Misses Schenck and
Thomas and herself to America for rest and recuperation. Her coming, however, was contingent
upon the arrival of Doctor Light and wife, with
Bishop Hott and a party of outgoing missionaries.
They (Doctor Light and wife) did not come, yet
she said: "I will not leave our missionaries without a physician. I shall feel as happy at Rotufunk
as if I had gone to America." She returned to her
work, satisfied with His way of doing things.
This to her seemed a trivial incident, but to those
who were very desirous to see her, it was a great
trial, and attested the love she had for her work.
The strain, however, was too great and her health
began to fail. Still she wrote: "This is my best
year in Africa," and "with a pang I remember that
in a few short weeks I shall have to leave my work
and go home."

She arrived in New York on Thanksgiving Day
of 1895. The high latitude, with her already en-
feebled condition, necessitated her staying indoors

for a greater part of the winter; in consequence thereof she did not get very far away from her home for several weeks. At last she ventured out, going to Terre Haute, Indiana, and stopping with a brother there some weeks more. Another venture, and she arrived at Decatur, Illinois, stopping several weeks with the writer. While here it was learned that she was undecided as to returning to Africa. Shortly after her arrival in Decatur she received a letter from Miss Eaton, one of the missionaries at Rotufunk, describing the trend of affairs, especially those with the new doctor, Miss Archer, with whom she had, while at home in Potsdam, some talk concerning the duties of a physician at Rotufunk. She seemed well pleased, and incidentally remarked that if certain conditions should obtain she might return. I think that her purpose to remain in America, if she had one, may date its first shock to that letter. From Illinois she went back to Terre Haute, Indiana, and with Miss C. C. Conley opened an office, for the practice of medicine, at 1531 North Eighth Street.

After some months here the need of a more desirable location was realized. One was sought and found on Third Street. While in that city she united with the Vigo Medical Society, attended the services at the United Brethren Church, and attended the meetings of the missionary society. She was not wholly satisfied with herself after embarking in this business enterprise, and, as I think, construed the lack of patronage to her being out of the line of duty, more than to anything else, and so regarded it as a call back to her missionary work. The association with Miss Conley was very agreeable, but not meeting with the success they both desired, at the end of six months the office was discontinued, Miss Conley returning to Cincinnati, Ohio, to work on the Cincinnati *Enquirer,* a position she had relinquished for the purpose of engaging in the practice of medicine, and Doctor Hatfield going to White Water, Wisconsin, to visit and attend an invalid sister, who, like herself, was a physician.

Having concluded to return to her loved work in Africa, she so notified the Board and met with them at their annual meeting at Lisbon, Iowa, in May, 1897. At this meeting she told her niece, Mabel Hatfield, daughter of the writer, that she was going to Africa to stay; that she did not expect to return; little thinking then that her stay would be so short, or that her discharge from duty would be so violent. God moves certainly in a mysterious way to accomplish his wise and beneficent purposes. We can only say, "Thy will be done."

A few months of preparation, a little talking here and there publicly, which always was a heavy cross to her, and the time for departure again arrived. One little incident occurred at a local meeting of the Board of Managers just prior to her leaving, which I shall speak of, simply to indicate the degree of heart she had in the work of saving the poor African. She was very desirous to own a full complement of surgical instruments, and not having the money to procure them, she asked a loan of fifty dollars from the society. It was immediately taken under advisement by the president, Mrs. L. K. Miller, and others, who, after consultation, returned and told the doctor that they could not loan her the money, but that they would make her a present of that amount. The announcement proved too much for her to withstand, and she completely collapsed, finding relief in a flood of tears. It is said that she afterward declared if there ever was a day in her life happier than when she received the notice that her first application to the Board was accepted, it was the one on which she received that fifty dollars, so generously given by the Board of Managers.

She sailed the second time from New York for Liverpool, October 2, 1897, in company with Mr. and Mrs. Cain, Miss Schenck, companions in martyrdom, and Mr. Ward; and Miss Mullen, in the employ of the Radical United Brethren Society, on board the *Lucania,* a Cunard liner, making close connection at Liverpool with the *Bagana,* a British steamer, bound for Freetown, where they landed October 23, making the voyage in less than a month. The voyage was uneventful, save the leaving of Miss Mullen at Liverpool, and the going ashore at Madeira. Freetown was reached in a storm. Was it significant? Did it forecast the exit? The Stars and Stripes and waving of handkerchiefs from the Yates & Porterfield building welcomed them, however, through the storm. When the fierceness of the storm abated, the mission boat with Mr. and Mrs. McGrew, Mr. and Mrs. King, and Miss Cronise on board, pushed out from the wharf and drew alongside the vessel and greeted the party with good cheer. Services were held at the home of Mr. Smart, of the Yates & Porterfield firm, on the evening of the twenty-fourth, by invitation. Mr. Kingman and Mr. Price, of the Sudan mission, were present. Rotufunk was reached in a day or two, and the party settled down to mission work, save the doctor and Mr. and Mrs. McGrew, who were preparing to go to the interior, to Taiama, in the Mendi country.

On the way to this latter place, overtaken by the rains, they sought shelter and rest in one of the villages, but found neither. The huts to which they were assigned were dilapidated and almost roofless, and they were compelled to sit up all night under their umbrellas. The doctor not being acclimated, could not endure the strain upon her physical resources, and she soon returned to Rotufunk for medical aid.

Her health never became fully restored, and her arduous duties proved too much for her impaired condition. She spent a little time at the Bethany Cottage, on Mt. Leicester. Again, constrained to accept medical treatment, she returned to Rotufunk, where she was that ill-fated third day of May. She was a member of the United Brethren class at Potsdam, Ohio, where it was her purpose to have her name remain, which, so far as I know, was done. How well she did her work the Board, in whose employment she died, will answer. Her work is done. The river is crossed, and although it was stormy and violent, rest and victory will be none the less sweet or less glorious. A martyr's crown is the privilege of but few, and He who sees and knows the heart and life makes no mistake in the award Let the tragic death of these heroes and heroines prove such an incentive to our church as to thrust her to the front in missionary endeavor in the years to come.

Ella Schenck.

Ella Schenck was the daughter of Rev. D. J. Schenck, of Auglaize Conference, and was born near Willshire, Ohio, January 30, 1866. Her mother died when she was but four years of age, but she always spoke most tenderly of the care and love of her second mother. Her educational privileges were limited and frequently interrupted, because of the itinerant life of the home; yet, by the watchful care of the mother, the children made commendable progress in study in the various schools they attended. She spent some time in Roanoke Classical Academy and at Eastern Indiana Normal School, where she graduated in the teachers' course in a shorter time than any other member of her class.

She subsequently took a course in stenography and typewriting in Sydney, and also acquired considerable knowledge of photography. She taught a number of schools, and with such success that not a word of complaint ever reached her parents. Though she loved home, she longed to do more for God and humanity in more needy fields. She often spoke of missionary work, and asked the consent of her parents to her entering the foreign field. Once she said to her father, "Would you consent to my going to Africa?" Scarcely weighing her question, he answered, "Yes, you can go." She cheerfully replied, "Well, I am going," and on September 23, 1891, in company with Doctor Hatfield and Elma Bittle, she sailed from New York on the Steamship *City of Chicago*. Her last words, sent back by the pilot that day, were: "May the God of

MISS ELLA SCHENCK.

love go with and keep us all true and faithful workers in the harvest fields, whether at home or in Africa. Farewell home, country, and friends! farewell until God chooses to reunite us either on earth or in heaven."

After a term of three and a half years in Africa and a rest of several years at home, she wrote the trustees of the Woman's Missionary Association: "I can no longer bear the responsibility of remaining in America, and I cheerfully offer myself for a second term in Africa." She again passed a favorable medical examination, was gladly accepted by the Board, and in company with Mr. and Mrs. Cain, Doctor Hatfield, and Arthur Ward, sailed October 1, 1897, and upon reaching Rotufunk took the position of her choice, the matronship of the Girls' Home, where she was so useful and so happy in her work. The following tribute from one well known, who worked with her on the field, will tell its story of her worth:

Mrs. Lida M. West writes of her: "Thinking of Ella Schenck, a life of consecration and devotion to God and humanity rises before me. The sweet impressions made on my mind, and that never left me as the years went by and our acquaintance ripened into intimacy, were first formed in her father's home in Lockington, Ohio, where I had gone to participate in her consecratory service. Her interest in the welfare and work of her father and mother, the loving helpfulness to brothers and sisters, especially the little brother, and the deep regrets of her many friends at her departure, made me realize what her home, church, and community had lost, and what the Woman's Missionary Association and Africa had gained. She went to Africa for Jesus' sake, loving the dear ones at home none the less, yet having a wealth of affection for those for whom she went to labor, and for whom she gave her life. Her earnest, loving heart and deep, sympathetic nature, found a ready response in the hearts of the natives. To the children she was always a friend; to the old, a confidant and comforter. A rich endowment of natural gifts coupled with grace eminently qualified her for the various positions which she occupied.

"During her first term her special work was in the school-room, where she rendered most excellent service. But in connection with this, and in it she delighted most, was the direct work with the people in their own homes, the work so dear to the heart of Miss Williams and laid down by her when she joined the company on high. Indeed, in was at home in the pulpit, and most happy in her relation as leader of the Sabbath morning seekers' class. She knew how to teach, exhort, and rebuke with all long-suffering. She was an ardent worker in Woman's Christian Temperance Union and Temperance Legion work and never failed to stand by in anything and everything that would help the people honor the Lord and hasten on his kingdom. She was generous to a fault. Time, strength, and money were freely yielded up even to her own detriment.

"Though so kind and gentle she was possessed of a strong will, making her a fearless denouncer of sin, and causing her to endure censure rather than yield a point that to her seemed right. 'She will make a good mother,' I said, on learning of her appointment to the Girls' Home. I am sure, as in other places, the Father's blessing would have been upon her work there.

"Associated with her in the field for two years, I loved her much, and I tenderly remember how in my own great sorrow she helped bear the burden and gave more than a sister's love.

"Her feelings on returning to Africa last fall are expressed in a personal letter written while on the way: 'I am in many respects glad to go back; more happy than when I first went, but the home-leaving was harder than before. However, I am trusting my Lord as I believe I have never trusted him before, and I firmly believe he is going just before me and choosing the way, and I am glad in him.

"'I shall go to the grave of your dear one and care for it, as I know you would do were you there —and it may be that my own resting-place shall be quite near; even so, if it please my Lord so to do with me.' Again she writes: 'I know how much you would like to be with us, and yet He who directs our paths knows where he needs us most. I go gladly. I have a deep abiding peace and comfort which makes and keeps me strong. I know, my dear (a term she so often used), you'll pray hard that much of the Master's will may be wrought in me.'

"These are her beautiful words, written when 'Frankie' and 'Elma' yielded up their beautiful lives for Africa's redemption: 'I can think of nothing that would make death more welcome than to meet it here, to die for these dear children as my Saviour died for me. It is the suffering and dying Saviour that melts the stony heart. So with us—that which our lives cannot do our deaths may do.' May it not be so, and did not he lead 'all the way, all the way?'"

LOWERY A. AND CLARA B. McGREW.

BY REV. W. L. BUNGER.

Lowery Allen McGrew was born November 5, 1858, at West Baltimore, Ohio, where he lived with his parents and worked on a farm until he was about twenty years of age. This manner of life gave him the healthy body and rugged constitution which afterward aided him to serve the Master in difficult fields. Though in early life his education was very much neglected, by hard study he prepared himself for teaching. It was in a school at Eldorado, Ohio, that he became acquainted with Miss Clara B. McCoy, whom he married August 9, 1883. The next year after his marriage he and his wife were converted in a meeting at West Baltimore, Ohio, and from this time seemed to begin the unfolding of God's plan in their lives, which plan is always larger and better than our own. In pursuance of His plan he entered the Seminary in 1886 and graduated in 1890, having done pastoral work the greater part of the time in connection with his school duties. After graduation he served Mt. Zion charge, Miami Conference, three years, and Cherry Grove charge until February 15, 1896, when he resigned to accept from the Woman's Missionary Board an appointment in the African field. Here he did faithful service for Christ until the tragic end came.

REV. AND MRS. L. A. MCGREW.

Mrs. McGrew was the daughter of pious parents, her father having been brought up in the Friends Church and her mother in the Methodist Episcopal Church, but after their marriage they became members of the United Brethren Church near Eldorado, Ohio, where in their country home many of the older ministers of Miami Conference were accustomed to share their hospitality.

Mrs. McGrew was born January 30, 1862, and lived a quiet, studious life until she was married and entered the Seminary. Her careful home training and early education, together with the Seminary course, eminently fitted her for the duties of a pastor's wife. She always shared in the burdens of the pastorate, often occupying the pulpit in the crowded seasons of work. She was particularly active in the missionary association work, and always had upon her heart the burden of the world's evangelization. In her letters to friends she expressed her willingness to serve Christ and the church wherever it was his will to place her. Now that she has given her life to the One she loved, may God raise up others to take her place in the ranks.

BY G. A. FUNKHOUSER, D.D.

Rev. and Mrs. L. A. McGrew entered the Seminary in September, 1886, graduated May, 1890, and were promoted to wear the martyr's crown, like Paul, May 9, 1898, at Taiama, West Africa.

They are the first of the graduates of the Seminary to be thus honored. True, Rev. Mr. West attended Seminary two years, gave his life to the risen Lord for service in Africa, and on the morning of the resurrection will come from the Dark Continent, but the names of Mr. and Mrs. McGrew will stand first on the roll of martyred graduates. Whose names next, our Father knows.

Mr. McGrew had been a successful school teacher. When called to preach he wished to enter at once upon the work. His presiding elder kindly told him he must first take a course in the Seminary. Mr. McGrew remonstrated, not wishing to spend the time and money necessary. The elder was firm, and the names of Mr. and Mrs. McGrew were on the roll of students. They located near the Seminary in their own property; staid four years, part of which time he served small charges as pastor.

He always referred with gratitude to the firmness of the elder, Dr. G. M. Mathews, which turned him into the Seminary for that equipment which made life mean more and opened larger fields of usefulness. Both were good students, conscientious, industrious, hard-working, and self-denying. They graduated in a class of thirteen.

After five years of efficient service in Miami Conference they saw the urgent appeal of the Woman's Board, offered themselves for service in Africa, and sailed March 28, 1896.

They never regretted their decision to serve in the front line where dangers were thickest, toil the hardest, because they saw the need was greatest. In letters to me Brother McGrew's utterances were always worthy, sometimes heroic. From his last to me, dated Bethany Cottage, February 18, 1898, I quote: "We spent three months at Taiama, then came here to take our vacation. The people of

Taiama were in quite a disturbed state while we were there, which made the work go very slowly. We are so apt to want the work to go in our own way and at our time, but the Lord knows best. The work is his, and that he will surely bless it there can be no doubt. When the night is darkest the pillar of fire is the brightest. Tell the students of the Seminary we are glad for the great interest they show in the mission work, and that some of them have their faces toward the heathen world. May the Lord bless you all."

Who of the Seminary alumni will with Isaiah say, "Here am I; send me"?

At first it did not appear right to speak of these two faithful workmen under one caption, but it seemed a necessity, because of lack of knowledge; and after maturer reflection it does not seem so incongruous. The two were blended into such a beautiful, harmonious union, one in aim, sympathy, aspiration, while supplementing each other in mental qualities. He was brave, she was cautious, both were very prudent and economical.

In a long journey through the Mendi country Mr. and Mrs. McGrew, Miss Cronise, and Superintendent King were my associates. Reaching Mongherri, Saturday noon, Mr. King and I resolved to go back over the road three or four miles to look for gold, having picked up some quartz containing some of the metal, as we came in. We found no more gold, but hearing a waterfall in the distance we went into the forest to find it. There we discovered and explored Lucile Falls. Night came on us, and we were lost in the jungle in trying to reach the path leading back to the village. We made a fire, and listened to the voices of the forest.

Toward midnight Mr. McGrew shouldered his gun and led a band of ten black men into the forest in search of us. He found us, pulled us out, and took us into camp before morning. We found the ladies in tears, but Mrs. McGrew's anxiety for her husband can never be forgotten by those who witnessed it.

Mr. King and I had fallen into a swamp in our efforts to get out of the woods, and were wet and chilly when we reached the city. I asked for something warm, but the fires were all out. Miss Cronise went to her medicine case and brought out a little phial (no larger than my little finger). It contained liquor, which I drank. Mrs. McGrew had a quarter of a pint of liquor. She gave Mr. King half a tablespoonful. Neither of us could get a drop more, for she informed us that Doctor Archer sent it along to be used only in case of a snake-bite. On inquiry, it was learned that all the balance of it returned from that long journey and reached Rotufunk in safety.

I cite this incident merely to emphasize one strong characteristic of both of these dear friends —their carefulness in managing the property and funds submitted to their care. Shortly before their death, Mr. McGrew wrote me that he had been able to save for the mission, during the eighteen months he was superintendent, $2,292.55 of the appropriations made for that period.

My associations with them were very pleasant, and they, with the others who have devoted their lives for the welfare of Africa, will ever live in my memory and affections.

RECOLLECTIONS.
BY MRS. LIDA M. WEST.

My acquaintance with the four of our beloved fallen missionaries, with whom I was associated in the field for more than two years, began in this country.

In 1891 in Lockington, Ohio, I had the privilege of participating in the service that publicly set apart for work in Africa Miss Ella Schenck.

The same year I first met Doctor Hatfield on the way to the Board meeting, held at Decatur, Illinois, where she received her appointment and was dedicated to her life work in the same field. In 1892, on the way to New York, after a night of broken rest, with a grip for a pillow, we lay half asleep, too weary to care that we were nearing the famous Horseshoe Bend. The day was just dawning when a tall, fine-looking man entered the car and a moment later was inquiring if we were the Wests. "I am Cain," he said. Mrs. Cain was in the sleeper. They had arisen early to see for the first time the mountains of Pennsylvania, and especially the Bend.

Mr. and Mrs. Cain were our companions to Africa. Doctor Hatfield welcomed us to Freetown, Sierra Leone, and Miss Schenck to our old home at Rotufunk.

I am asked for personal recollections of these four. Sadly I turn back to the happy past and think and live over again the days when we were all together as one family.

The hope so fondly cherished of one day joining them again on the field is gone. But there is left the glad anticipation of a part with them, by and by, in the higher service in which they are now engaged.

In Mr. and Mrs. Cain there was that happy combination of natural qualities, culture and grace that not only produces a beautiful home life, but forms the basis of earnest, successful Christian work. How nobly they planned and labored side by side, in church and school and home, and everywhere as workmen that needed not to be ashamed! Her chosen work and, perhaps, her best was in the school-room, while he threw himself with a little extra enthusiasm into the industrial. How well I remember the delight with which the different kinds of clay were gathered and molded into brick; the anxiety, as he watched over the first little kiln, and the rejoicing over the bright prospect for the future, as seen through the small number that stood the test of fire and water. How often we smiled as he came running up the steps of the Girls' Home, his face all aglow, so eager to communicate some bright, new thought or plan that had just come to him. His love and zeal sometimes exceeded his physical strength (not an uncommon thing for a missionary), and now I find myself wondering whether the little monument he erected in loving memory of dear faithful Daddy Queen has shared the common fate of all our precious belongings. It was formed of stone and cement, with the little slate bearing the inscription. The last finishing touches of love were given at half past ten at night; then followed those weeks of serious illness that came so near closing up his life work.

Brother Cain was our pastor. Tenderly let me recall those hallowed Sabbath services in the beloved old chapel at Rotufunk. I see them all in their accustomed places; Miss Thomas at the organ; in our hands "Hymns for the Sanctuary." They naturally open at page 346, Nos. 864 and 865, for are they not his favorite hymns, and so seldom omitted at the morning service—"My Jesus as thou wilt," and "Thy way, not mine, O Lord." So beautiful then—how significant now:

> "Take Thou my cup, and it
> With joy or sorrow fill,
> As best to thee may seem;
> Choose thou my good and ill."

O consecrated heart, God gave thee his best and brightest choice.

Of Mrs. Cain I have also only beautiful memories. I never think of her but I see that peculiarly sweet, winning smile and a group of little black faces. She was not only mother to all the little boys in the mission, but their idol as well. They loved her and were never so happy as when around her door or sitting at her feet. She must know all their joys and hear all their little palavers. If she smiled on them, patted their little curly heads, and said, in her own sweet way, "Oh, never mind," their little hearts "lay down" (were comforted). How helpful she was to us all, so loving and kind and good.

Perhaps no department of missionary work gives room for greater discouragement or need of more patience than the medical. In itself there is little that is pleasant or desirable. The heart grows sick amid the awful scenes of suffering and want and death, and then fires with indignation at the cruel treatment given these poor, helpless, distressed ones by their own friends, and at the utter indifference and positive disobedience to the orders of the faithful physician, who carries the responsibility of the life, often causing a complete failure of her work.

There must be a vision of the poor suffering ones and of Jesus, the compassionate Saviour. This alone can give strength and enthusiasm to the work. Such a vision, I believe, was given Doctor Hatfield in the years past, when her preparation for Africa began. She was always ready, no matter as to time, place, or distance, if some one needed her.

Then I remember her intense anxiety for the lives and health of the missionaries. Some of the usual morning salutations as one after another came to the dining-room for the early cup of tea, were, "Did you rest well through the night?" "How is your temperature, normal? "Feeling better?" "All right, are you?" with a keen, quick glance into the face to detect the first indication of fever. Poor doctor! how many heartaches she must have had over our imprudences, necessary or otherwise.

She grieved deeply over the loss of our faithful workers, and after the death of Mr. West, urging strongly my return for a time to this country, she piteously added, "Oh, it will kill me if I have to bury any more missionaries."

One of her ideals for the future was a force of trained nurses and physicians, gathered from the mission boys and girls. When our own George King, who had been her assistant for two years, and who had just fitted up a little medicine-chest and taken it to the Boys' Home to begin the practice of medicine on the very day when he became ill, and when in another week he was in the city where they have no need of a physician, for the inhabitants thereof never say I am sick, the blow fell with crushing weight on the doctor.

She had also learned Solomon's secret, that "a merry heart doeth good like a medicine." And many a witty saying and hearty laugh turned the tide of some little happening, or cheered into hope the discouraged one. She never failed to see the ridiculous side. She was strikingly original. A Bundoo woman having died, for three successive days and nights the women of the Bundoo Society kept up their dance in honor of the dead. This consisted in marching back and forth from Rotufunk below us to the Tartar above, clapping hands, singing, and dancing, keeping time to the shaking of calabashes and beating of drums. The road being so near the mission house there was no sleep for the missionaries. Doctor appealed to the chief, but without effect. By two o'clock in the morning she had her plan matured. Taking the skeleton (which she had been cleaning up), she placed it on the gate-post, then hiding in the grass, she awaited developments. The moon was shining brightly; there was a sudden stop in the procession, a few moments of perfect stillness, followed by a loud burst of laughter. Some one had seen it before, probably as it hung from the chandelier in the chapel when the doctor delivered her lectures on health and heredity. Doctor arose, acknowledged she was beaten, joined in the laugh, and then received the promise that the missionaries should not again be disturbed, a promise which they kept for that time.

Doctor was a very busy woman. Going into her room for a little chat might interrupt the special work in which she was engaged, but there on the table stood the ever-present quinine bottle, and that was just the opportunity for a new supply of those deftly-made tissue-paper balls that no missionary cares to enlarge upon.

As one who came "not to be ministered unto, but to minister."

"Inasmuch as ye have done it unto one of the least of these, my brethren, ye have done it unto me."

Blessed one! thy ministry is ended. Enjoy thy rich reward.

When Miss Schenck consecrated her beautiful life to the evangelization of Africa she placed upon the altar of sacrifice rare qualities of mind and heart. It is difficult to say just where the light shone brightest.

To have seen her in the school-room one would have thought her life was bound up in the advancement of her pupils. When leader of the Sabbath morning seekers' class every joy, every sorrow, and every temptation of those under her care was fully entered into. I loved this class from long connection with it, and because of the insight it gave into the inner life of the people. When no longer able to attend because of other duties, how I appreciated the testimonies she so faithfully reported. When among the children she seemed to have found her place. They knew she had room in her great sympathetic heart for them all, and to her their secrets were freely revealed.

But what she loved most was coming in close contact with the strangers in the town and the people in their homes. It was the work so dear to the heart of Miss Williams, and who was better fitted to take it up than she, for in many ways she was so like our own beloved Frankie. Fearless in denouncing sin in the presence of the Mohammedan, the slave dealer, and the Porroh man; skillful in the word of God; tender and patient to the slave, the aged, and the suffering; and though the former may have helped to take the precious life at last, the latter will bathe the spot where she now sleeps with tears of deepest affliction.

Most sacred are the memories that cluster around those last days that marked the closing up of Mr. West's life, and of my own work in Africa. Only the most tender ministries for him; but who to minister to them in that last sad hour? Only the most loving sympathy for me, but not deeper nor truer than that which filled the hearts of the dear boys who stood by weeping while the cruel war-boys did their awful work.

Just one year ago in Lisbon, Iowa, I looked upon their faces, listened to their voices in song and prayer, sat at table with them, talked of Africa, the happy past and the inviting future, and gave the last good-by, sorrowing most of all that I should be left behind. Oh, who could have dreamed that so great a calamity could have befallen us within so short a time!

"In memory of John Coleridge Patteson, D.D., whose life here was taken by men for whom he would gladly have given it," is the inscription upon the tall iron cross which marks the place of his martyrdom in Melanesia. No better or truer thing can be said of our own beloved martyrs.

"We cannot see, but the Father bids us trust him. We may not know, but he bids us believe him. We dare not stop, for he bids us with his own dear voice go on." Our hearts respond to these words of Miss Schenck, and we will, stepping over the graves of our beloved ten, go on until the light of the gospel shall shine into every dark corner of Africa.

Of this noble band Rev. J. R. King says: "In memory's hall, as in a gallery of art, hang many beautiful pictures. Some are valued highly because of their worth as masterpieces; others, because of their peculiar associations. In my memory the pictures of our martyred missionaries are cherished for both reasons mentioned. The memory of their lives floats back to one as the cool, fragrant breeze on a hot August evening, making one forget the selfishness and the base sinfulness with which he is surrounded. To the world and humanity they were valuable. Each one possessed special elements of natural endowment and adaptation for the work in which they were engaged; and they all had by careful preparation fitted themselves for their chosen work. But to the church they represented in the thick of the fight against heathenism and superstition, they were especially valuable.

Like beautiful stones, skillfully chiseled and shaped, they have been placed in the structure of Africa's civilization and evangelization which God is rearing. Even though they be foundation stones, will not their worth be felt and the beauty of their lives realized? To me they are priceless; associated in the work, the memory of each one is cherished as a heavenly benediction. Brave and loyal to Christ and the truth, in the face of discouragement and persecution, they present to us splendid examples of consecration and devotion. The prominent traits that to me seemed to stand out in their characters were:

"Brother Cain, a holy zeal for the regions beyond, with unselfish consideration for others' comfort. Mrs. Cain, a calm and serene disposition, so marked as to quiet the waves of a stormy nature in a very wide circle; also with high ideals of character which she sought to attain in those whom she taught.

"Brother McGrew, careful, painstaking, with a remarkable devotion to his work, and a practical turn that made him invaluable to the mission. Mrs. McGrew, with a devotion so strong as to overcome natural timidity, and a great capacity for work.

"In Miss Schenck was a consecration so complete as to remove her every act far from self-interest, and a sweetness of life that would help the heathen a long way to understand Christ.

"Doctor Hatfield had a practical turn, with intense Christlike sympathy for suffering, and was also remarkable for her trust in God. Her favorite promise was, 'All things work together for good,' etc.

"Doctor Archer was also very practical, with an intense love for her profession, and, not simply as a profession, but as an avenue of approach to the spiritual work for which she was so well adapted by a Christlike love for souls. In ability, so many sided that her loss will be hard to replace.

"These special points indicate something of the loss we sustain, but the fragrance from their lives ought to enrich many lives. A perfect number— our seven martyred missionaries. There is a mystery overshadows the church in this loss. But to me it seems that God means to teach us lessons rich and beautiful, that the spirit of self-sacrifice and loving devotion may more completely guide our lives. This rich effusion of precious blood will surely bring forth a bountiful harvest of souls redeemed from Africa's darkness and superstition."

The following paper was written by Rev. Isaac N. Cain, and reached me shortly before his much-lamented death. It reveals the appreciative spirit of the writer, as well as the noble life of the one about whom he writes.

Rev. Richard N. West and His Work in Africa.

BY REV. ISAAC N. CAIN.

Very few men have held a more exalted position in the minds of the people of the United Brethren Church than Rev. R. N. West. Of humble birth, he worked his way by perseverance and true industry, to a fitness for life's work and finally to a most enviable success and glorious end. He was born in Jay County, Indiana, December 25, 1850, of Quaker parents, who were active Abolitionists.

Rev. R. N. West.

This may account, in a great measure, for his sympathy for the African race.

Very early in life he manifested a genius for the study of medicine, and acquired considerable knowledge of that science, which was of much value to him in after years in his missionary work in Africa.

At the age of twenty years he began to teach school, and continued to be identified with the educators of his community, part of the time in the capacity of a teacher, and part of the time seeking better equipment, until he was thirty years of age. With his conversion, which occurred in 1877, he felt the call to the African missionary work and soon began special preparation, joining the Auglaize Conference in 1880, and also beginning his work in the Union Biblical Seminary the same year.

In the summer of 1882 (June 22) the trustees of the Woman's Missionary Association appointed Mr. West to the superintendency of their missions in Bompeh District, on the west coast of Africa. At the same time Miss Lida Miller, who had been a student in the Seminary with Mr. West, was appointed to the same field. These two were married in August, 1882, and on the second of October of the same year, they started on their first voyage from New York City to Sierra Leone. They took passage on the old *Liberia*, and were two months on the sea.

The arrival of Mr. West and his good companion at Rotufunk, the headquarters of the mission, brought new impulses and new hopes to the work already established, which work was at that time under the direction of the noble missionary, Mrs. Mair.

Mr. West planned immediate extension, and that plan has characterized the work of Bompeh Mission ever since. Extension has been slow, but it has ever been the spirit and impulse among the native workers, as well as among the missionaries. Both the evangelistic and educational work were advanced and strengthened by his presence. He set about the task of systematizing every department of the institution over which he had charge. A revival spirit characterized the work from the very first, which continued to grow, and finally culminated in the great revival at Rotufunk in 1890. This revival spread to the out-stations, affecting hundreds of people, and its influence is still felt in all the community.

The personal character of Mr. West was ably portrayed by Miss Ellen Groenendyke in the *Woman's Evangel* of November, 1894. His was a cheerful disposition, without any display of levity, with a power and disposition to be helpful to others under all circumstances. He had a firm faith in God's providing care. We have often heard him say, when tried by great difficulties, "God reigns." This was his watchword. He thoroughly believed in the conversion of the African people. Even in the midst of disappointments he was faithful in carrying out the command of the Master, "Go ye therefore, and make disciples of all the nations." He was of a disposition to rejoice over his successes and forget his reverses.

The many instances which called forth the true heroism in our brother would make a book, the reading of which would stir our hearts and spur us on to nobler efforts for the advancement of the cause which he so much loved and for which he gave his life. On land and sea he was always composed and fearless in times of danger. In time of war and ravaging disease he trusted and pushed right on. His appearance was liable to give one an impression of frailty rather than of force and strong will, but his frail tabernacle of clay was no criterion of the hero-soul which dwelt within.

Looking about for the results of the labors of Brother West, we are not disappointed. In the twelve years of his management of Bompeh Mission we have seen the growth and development from a small beginning to an institution which is a credit to the church which he represented, and the colony within the borders of which he labored.

In the twelve years two permanent chapels were completed and a third was almost ready for dedication, one large school building, a commodious girls' home, a boys' home, one mission house, besides a number of additional buildings, were completed. All these were built in modified European style. Besides these there were built a number of large native houses for the use of the various itinerants. When we consider that much of the time our brother had to act in the capacity of doctor, pastor, teacher, farmer, bookkeeper, and treasurer, and also, when we consider that the forces of the climate are all against the white man, and that methods of transportation are slow in Africa, and that he made many important trips about the country, we can but wonder at what he accomplished.

In the twelve years he took two vacations, spending about two years away from the field.

The farther we are removed from the mark on the dial of time when we last saw his face on earth, the more strongly are we convinced of the real stability of the character of his work in Africa. Situated here at Rotufunk, we look out every day upon the monuments of the untiring zeal of this man of God and his noble companion.

The Girls' Home, where the native girls are trained for lives of usefulness among their people, is a monument to his memory as well as to that of some of his associates. Out of this home have gone several girls to help in building up Christian homes in this land where really Christian homes are sadly rare. The same may be said of the boys' home.

The young men who were children under Brother and Sister West are now our most efficient native force.

These institutions cannot now be measured in their value. The eternal records alone will reveal in the "last time" what a man with a high and good purpose, with an intense love for his work, and with thorough consecration, can accomplish.

The territory in which Mr. West was placed is, providentially, the finest in this part of Africa, and he was so thoroughly active that the ground is held and our territory has been greatly protected and enlarged through the interest he took in interior work. It was through his first trip to the interior, in 1889, and a second projected by Mr. Sage, under his direction, that we gained and still hold, such a vantage ground in the Mendi country. This has enabled the Parent Board to claim a district and enter upon the farther interior work in adjoining territory to that of the Woman's Missionary Association, and thus our forces as a church will be able, by divine assistance, to move up in solid phalanx to the battle of the Lord.

Shortly after Mr. West visited Bo, in 1888, he wrote a letter, which appeared in the *Woman's Evangel,* telling of the need of the great Mendi towns. That letter was the means used of God to turn the mind of the writer of this article toward Darkest Africa and to cause him to give himself for service in that needy field, and when five years later it was his privilege, as an amateur missionary, to accompany the veteran to the interior, he could but feel that he was being shown into the very field of his life-work by the same one who had been instrumental in deciding him to come.

Not only did his letters inspire many people at home to come out to Africa as missionaries, but it is a fact well worth our notice that many were inspired to greater liberality to the cause of Christ. The Mendi fund was started by the Woman's Missionary Association, and hundreds of dollars raised as a result of the interest awakened through Mr. West's determined purpose to move out into the interior of Africa. That purpose, though not carried out in his lifetime, has been the signal for others to actually begin a work, noble and grand, and which cannot fail to be far-reaching in its results. The work is being planted now by missionaries, and young native men and women, who still revere the memory of that faithful missionary and true friend of the African people.

His last sermon at Rotufunk, in September, 1894, was an intense exhortation to be obedient to the commission of the Saviour. On the 22d of the same month he fell on sleep, and as we said the last words of respect and resignation over his remains, in the waning light of a tropical day, we could not but feel that a life worthy of imitation had been lived before us; and while we sorrowed with the dear one left behind, we felt that a faithful child of the King had that day been freed from the bondage of the flesh and had passed triumphantly through the gate into the city of our God, there to dwell forever with the Lord.

A strong and beautiful life had been lived, and the end was victory.

FRANCES WILLIAMS.
BY MRS. MARY NEASE KEISTER.

Frances Williams, the first missionary in the United Brethren Church to be promoted from the foreign field, was the youngest daughter of J. W. and Mary Jane Compton Williams. Her father having been married three times, she had two older half sisters, Mrs. Ellen Knowlton and Mrs. Colonel Penny; two full brothers; two younger half brothers, and one sister; also a stepsister near her age.

Frances was born in Francisville, Indiana, April 29, 1860. Her mother died when she was four years of age, but an elder sister (Sadie) cared for her. She dated her first religious impressions back to that early date, for she felt then that if she were not a Christian she could not go to heaven and would never see her mother again. But it was not until she was twenty years old that she gave her heart to Jesus. One Saturday night, December

18, 1880, during a gracious revival conducted by Rev. S. W. Keister, at Union City, Indiana, she was gloriously saved.

She had been at the altar of prayer for three nights, but being exceedingly bashful, she feared to trust the Lord. Near ten o'clock that night, with but few of her friends kneeling around her at the altar, she was persuaded to uncover her face and, looking upward, to overcome the "man-fearing spirit." Like a flash of lightning the blessing came. She sprang to her feet, saying, "Hallelujah; Praise the Lord!" and without waiting to greet any one she started for the door, near which sat her sister waiting for her. Jennie saw her coming, saw what had happened, and slipped out of the door. Without her shawl, which she had dropped at the altar, Frankie followed, praising God aloud all the way home. The next morning, at the nine o'clock class-meeting, with a beaming face she was first to testify, and during her Christian life of twelve years she was exceptionally quick and prompt in testimony, a marvel to those who knew of her timidity before her conversion. That day she united with the church, and July 10, 1881, she and eight others were baptized by immersion by her pastor. She used to say often, "Brother Keister! you took me into church, baptized me, now you are to marry me and preach my funeral." She was not a little disappointed when her consecration service to missionary work was read by another, for she said, "This is my marriage and I wanted Brother Keister to read it."

About eight months after her conversion, at a camp-meeting held near the same place, for the promotion of holiness, she consecrated her all to the Lord, and on the way home, in a crowded omnibus, she received the baptism of power, which was the secret of her happy life. She had a secret desire to be a missionary, but saw so many difficulties in the way that she feared to mention it to any one. One day her pastor's wife came in where she was sewing (she was a nice dressmaker) and found her interested in the *Woman's Evangel* she had been reading. This brought up the subject, and she said, "Frankie! wouldn't you like to be a missionary?" "O Sister Keister," and the big tears fell from her bright, blue eyes, "do you think I could? Why, I should be the happiest person living, if I might." From that time hope began to spring up, and life had new possibilities, which she had feared to dream of, for she was so unconscious of her ability, so humble.

Her want of a better education seemed her greatest hindrance, but when it was known that she wanted to go to school, God provided helpful friends for her. Mr. and Mrs. John Mackey gave her a room in their own house, to use for dressmaking, and while Sister Mackey helped her much with her needle, she helped her more with her prayers, sympathy, and her godly conversation. But with her needle she found it slow work to lay up money to go to college. Soon Brother Albert Lambert, who with his good wife have helped so many with their means and blessings, believed that with a little assistance Frankie could soon understand bookkeeping well enough to keep the books in his warehouse. She did so, and while it meant better wages, it was also a preparation for that which

Miss Frances Williams.

afterward made her so valuable to the Woman's Missionary Association as business manager in Africa. When Brother Lambert built their new home, one nice room was called "Frankie's room." To it she came during her vacations, and she entered into their plans, shared their joys and sorrows, as one of their own daughters. When Jesus comes, these friends will receive rewards as those who "did it unto me." From there she went to Otterbein University, where by great economy, such as boarding herself, borrowing books, etc., with gifts of clothing from friends and some help from the church, she spent three years. She was very appreciative, and always worthy of the confidence friends had in her. She was a model Christian girl in school, and since, when mothers there want to say the best things of their daughters, they say, "She is our Frankie Williams." She was loyal to Otterbein. While in Africa she wrote Mrs. West, then in the homeland, "You will go to Otterbein University, dear old place! That to me is the dearest spot on earth, outside of Africa."

Later, she spent two years in the Moody Bible Training School for Workers, in Chicago. Here, in connection with her studies, she did much real missionary work among the Chinese, the colored people, and the poor. These all loved her. The Chinese made her presents of their painted china and beautiful embroidery, etc.

Her work was so acceptable that other churches made her good offers for the foreign field, which were no small temptation to her, when she was so anxious to go, and her own church so long getting ready to send her. It was only her loyalty to her church that saved her to it. When the Board of Managers was in session in Harrisburg, Pennsylvania, in 1889, she felt it must be that she should be sent then, for she had expected to go the year before. She gave herself one whole day to fasting and prayer, and when the word came that she was to go, she said, "I am so glad I'm going to Africa." If friends tried to sympathize with her, she said so joyfully, "If you had wanted anything all your life, would you be sorry when you got it?"

Her consecration service with that of Miss Patterson, who went to China, was held in First Church, Dayton, Ohio, July 7, 1889. Her farewell service was held in the United Brethren Church at Union City, Indiana, October 3, 1889. Rev. S. W. Keister, her former pastor, Rev. S. B. Ervin, the resident pastor, and Rev. W. J. Pruner, a former pastor of Miss Groenendyke, took part in these services. At this meeting she first saw Miss Groenendyke, who had been appointed to go to Africa with her, and, of course, was anxious to see first what she would look like. A shadow of disappointment flashed over her face, for that day Miss Groenendyke was not prepossessing in appearance. She, that afternoon, had separated from her friends in Indiana, and her eyes and nose were swollen from weeping. But Frankie never said a word, for she was too good to say aught against the "Lord's anointed," and before she slept that night she was very, very glad that she had not, for in the evening meeting Miss Groenendyke's first public sentence, so strong, representing so much character, went like a thunderbolt through the audience, captivating every interested heart. From that hour Frankie loved her most dearly. The next ten days were full of buying and packing, receiving calls and addressing large meetings in Dayton, Ohio. Their trunks were packed in the home of the writer, and their leave-taking was as happy as that of two school-girls off for a vacation. How could we be sorry when they were so glad? They left Dayton on the morning of the fourteenth and sailed on the *Teutonic,* October 16, 1889, at 10:40 A. M., and these were the parting words: "We are afloat at last. I was never happier in my whole life. The Ninety-first Psalm comes to me o'er and o'er. Ellen Groenendyke."

"We are cut loose from America. Boat fine, morning beautiful. The Lord is my light and salvation. Praise the Lord. We are happy in him, and longing to be in Africa. Yours for loving service for our King. Frankie Williams."

Arrived in Liverpool, October 23. Miss Groenendyke had been very ill, indeed she had crossed the Atlantic without seeing it. But Frankie writes: "Am so well and so thankful. Have been on deck every day." On board she became quite intimate with a Miss Field, who was returning to her home in London, a worker among the poor in that city, and she said: "Whether we walk, or talk, sit and read our Bibles, or kneel in prayer, we find ourselves drawing near our Father and Friend. That the Master has given me such deep content and so great joy, greatly surprises me. I am so glad we are sailing for Africa." Through the kindness of Mr. Mills they were able to get passage on the *Sherbro,* which sailed October 26; were very much crowded, but nothing unusual happened.

Miss Groenendyke said, "Spent the time in reading, talking, walking, music, eating, and sleeping in larger or smaller quantities." Made their first landing at the Grand Canary, November 2, and at Freetown, November 12, after a voyage of twenty-seven days from New York. Were met on board the vessel by Mr. and Mrs. West and George Keister. Stayed at Freetown until Thanksgiving Day. Took the A. L. Billheimer boat for Rotufunk. Mrs. West and Miss Groenendyke were very seasick, but Frankie said: "I know nothing of it but by observation, and I am satisfied with that, and when I consider how heartily I have enjoyed my four meals each day, I am not surprised that I have gained eight pounds in six weeks. Reached Rotufunk at two o'clock in the morning, went to bed, after greeting the boys and girls who were all up at that time in the night to see us, but arose early the next morning to see Rotufunk by daylight. I walked the piazza and looked at the Girls' Home, the Boys' Home, the frame for the new school-building. I could not keep back the tears. [Mr. West said she shouted.] My heart was filled with gratitude to God for hearing my prayers and bringing me here. In all my dreams of being a missionary I never pictured such pleasant surroundings as I find here. I shall be so glad when I may take my Bible and go from house to house, and show from it the true and living way to the lost. *I am so happy to be here."*

Her description of her first Christmas was real, but as she told of decorating the chapel with bouquets, palms, and ferns, gathering fresh roses to wear with their white dresses to the services, it was, to us, an American Children's Day rather than Christmas. Then she adds, "This was the busiest and happiest Christmas of my life."

During the Board meeting held the following May in the Summit Street United Brethren Church, of Dayton, Ohio, special prayer services were held by the missionaries in Africa for a revival. Frankie had a Sabbath-school class made up of policemen and traders, in whose souls she was much interested, and she had talked to the traders plainly on the temperance question. On Saturday morning, as usual, she went down town to see her flock. She saw a Mr. Coker, a man past fifty, quite intelligent and very determined, selling rum from his piazza. They sat down together and had a long talk. After a little silence he called his wife to get a man to bring out the rum and gin. He had two demijohns of rum and twenty-four bottles of gin; he ordered them carried to the stream, and he himself began breaking the bottles, unsealing the demijohns, and pouring out the drink. Such a thing had never been known in that part of Africa before, and the excitement ran high. The people begged by the most pitiful gestures for just one taste, but Frankie appealed to the policemen standing by to see that the order was carried out.

This is from her diary: "The men in my class were dealing in slaves, living in polygamy, buying, selling, and drinking rum; smoking, chewing, and trading in tobacco; but from the first they seemed interested in the Bible; glad to have me talk to them, though they did not like all I said. But I never had a class in America that I was so interested in. I prayed for them every day and visited them almost as often. The burden for their salvation grew heavier every day. On Wednesday night preceding the Saturday above referred to, it seemed as if I should die if the Lord did not come soon and save some of my class All night I wrestled in prayer, and as I wept, I felt as Jeremiah did when he said, 'Oh that my head were waters, and mine eyes a fountain of tears, that I might weep day and night for the slain of the daughter of my people!' Mr. Coker was away from home that night, but returned on Friday, and I hunted him up and gave him the Word of God on the liquor question. Finally he said, 'Missus, you convince me.' I urged him to act at once on his convictions; he offered excuses, but they were all met by the Word of the Lord. At last he agreed to sell no more, but would keep what he had and give it to his landlord and others with whom he had to deal. Then, 'Woe unto him that giveth his neighbour drink' was quoted. Then he said, 'Oh, missus, lef the matter for now.' I said, 'Now is the accepted time.' I knew God was in our midst and his Spirit striving with him. I ceased talking and prayed silently and earnestly. In a moment (it seemed many) he called his wife to get a man to 'pull' the rum from his house and throw it out. One look at Mr. Coker convinced us that he was glad, and I said we ought to thank God for what he had done. We knelt down and I tried to tell the Father of the gratitude that filled my heart, but no words could express it. While singing, 'Praise God from whom all blessings flow,' Thomas Hallowell came up. I told him what was done. He said, 'When I hear it my hair stand up. I shake and sweat.' There was great rejoicing in the mission that day, and I wondered who had received the greater blessing, Mr. Coker or I. Later in the day Thomas visited him again and said, 'Oh! the man happy for true. His face shines. Plenty people come to his house and he talk to all of them.' The next day he came to our meeting and was converted."

This was the beginning of the greatest revival Rotufunk has ever seen. It lasted four weeks. No accurate account of the number of conversions could be kept. Many persons were passing through the place, who went on. Mr. and Mrs. West, Mr. and Mrs. Sage, Miss Groenendyke, and Miss Williams were the missionaries there at that time, and all wrote of it and referred to it again and again. Mrs. West said, "The very air seemed charged with the Spirit. Convictions were so powerful that men's knees knocked together so hard that they could hardly walk to the altar." One of Frankie's class said, "For a long time I have had a bone in my heart, but now it hurts me harder than ever." Later, when asked, "Does Jesus save you now," he said with a joyous laugh, "Yes; I feel here that Jesus pull sickness from my heart. God is so sweet."

It was during this meeting that Pa Sourri, the powerful old chief, upwards of eighty years of age, came in to the morning meeting, and fell headlong across the altar so heavily that it seemed as if his neck must be broken. He had had an all-night struggle with "two persons," one for good, the other for evil. A repetition of Saul of Tarsus. He was converted, and put away his many wives, except "Mammy Mary." He died in 1897, and told Dr. Mary Archer, who talked with him about his soul, that he was trusting in Jesus, and God would take care of him whether he lived or died. He wanted to be buried from the church, but his heathen friends forbade it. Mr. West said of the revival, "Last week Frankie and her faithful boys scored a wonderful victory. Two old men, a wife, daughter and granddaughter came to Rotufunk on business. Not one of them had ever heard a word of the gospel. Frankie saw them and talked to them about salvation. The next day found them earnestly praying for themselves. One of the women took the 'sebbie' from her neck and gave it to Frankie, (there had been nothing said to her about that) who told her to keep it as maybe her heart would go back to it again. She said, No; for though it had cost her the price of a slave, since she had Jesus she did not want anything else. All five were clearly converted in the little mud hut down town, and the next morning at prayers gave their names and testimony as clear as one could wish."

Frankie and Miss Groenendyke went to Palli after this to assist Mr. Johnson, and she writes, "The scene was indescribable. Every seat in the house was a mourner's bench, and every soul, except the little band of workers, a seeker. Thirty-seven were converted in ten days. Oh, that we could give you some idea of the condition of the people here. If you could only hear the testimonies of the men and women who thank the God of missions for sending them the Word, and say so pitifully that their fathers and mothers never heard it, and beg us to go to other towns and tell all their people. It is work we cannot do that kills us faster than that we do. But perhaps some of the dear friends wonder whether we girls have been homesick since we came to Africa. I want to tell you no! no! never for one moment. Dear as my friends, home, and native land are to me, it would be harder to leave the work of my Master and King here than it was to leave home ten months ago. The blessed peace that Christ has given me ever since the night he saved me has never been so deep and sweet as to-day, and I should like to write three columns of praise to God for his wonderful works and words and ways. But I haven't the space, so I think I shall ask you all to join us in singing the doxology, and I shall say, Amen."

January 25, 1891, during the session of the West African Conference, Frankie, with Miss Groenendyke, Mrs. West, Mr. S. F. Morrison, and Jacob Miller, Jr., were ordained by Bishop Kephart. After this she administered the Lord's Supper, preached, and baptized. In a private letter to Mrs. Dora Lambert she says, "Last Sabbath morning, at the close of the service, two men came forward for baptism. It was my duty to furnish them Christian names. As I stood for a moment my mind flew like lightning back to my home church, and I thought of two of the best men I ever knew, my first pastor and my class-leader, and I gave the men the names Samuel Keister and Albert Lambert."

Need I say that the mat upon which she then stood, and which was given by Mrs. West to Rev.

S. W. Keister and family after her death, is greatly prized? During Brother Miller's stay in Africa she was made business manager, and kept the books of the mission. This was a sore disappointment to her, for all her plans were how she might give more time to visitation among the Mohammedans there. One day she noticed how much time it took to comb her hair, and said: "That would be an hour more every week. I'll have it cut, and have that much more for my Mohammedans. I shall let it grow again before father sees me." Her knowledge of the Scriptures and skill in handling the Sword of the Spirit made her very successful among that class of persons. Later she writes, "I submit, and hope my bookkeeping time may be to me as Moses' sheep-keeping time was to him." She was much cheered by the coming of the trio of girls in the fall of 1891, and welcomed them because of their ability and Rotufunk's need. Her love for the people never flagged and her letters ended with "Yours for service in Africa." Then, when we thought all was well, like a clap of thunder from a clear sky, the cablegram: "Frankie is dead. Miller. Rotufunk."

An editorial in the *Woman's Evangel* said, "Her joy in her work was boundless, and the good she has done can never be summed up by mortal, and we wept and waited to know more, yea, all we could know of the last hours of our precious one, who headed the list of those who laid down their lives for Africa in Africa." From her last letter we have this, "I shall be so glad when Mr. and Mrs. West return, that I may go back to my former work."

"July 9. I could not have better health anywhere than I am having here. If our Lord tarries, it seems to me the last year of my first term will be the best. I do not like to think that in autumn of next year my first term will be up. I rejoice more and more in him and feel that his loving kindness is better than life. Ah! it is sweet to toil for Jesus anywhere, but I think there is no place where work is so fascinating as here."

The letters describing her sickness, death, and burial, are from Miss Bittle, Doctor Hatfield, and Miss Groenendyke. "Frankie had always been so well, that we thought her fever-proof. Full of plans for the Master's work, losing no opportunities for giving the Word of life to the people, she went about her duties as usual up to within a few hours of her departure. Saturday evening she was weighed, and her weight was 107 pounds. It pleased her to think she weighed two pounds more than Doctor Hatfield. Sabbath morning at breakfast she did not look well, but said, 'I am only tired.' She had held the early morning meeting and had gone down-town to talk to the people before this. She attended the eleven o'clock service, but stayed in the chapel with Miss Bittle until Sabbath school at 1:30. Taught her class, and at dinner said she felt as well as usual, and thought she would attend the evening service. But after the last bell had rung, the doctor was surprised to find her standing on the piazza, and took her to her room and gave her quinine. She had no fever. Next morning she said she felt 'tip-top,' and went to the office and wrote all day, mostly business letters; the doctor did not see her until four o'clock. Said she had no fever. But when the doctor took her temperature it was 103.8 degrees. She said, 'Miss Williams, you must go to bed at once.' Frankie said, 'Before dinner? Why, I 'm hungry, and haven't an ache or pain.' She laughed and joked while Miss Schenck and the doctor put her to bed in Miss Schenck's room. They told her now to keep quiet. She smiled sweetly and said, 'All right; if you think best.' At dinner she did not care for anything to eat; at eight o'clock had vomited, was quieter at eleven, but at 1 a. m. she showed alarming symptoms, and the doctor knew if these could not be checked, the case was hopeless. She and Miss Schenck worked with her until two. She was conscious up to this time, but said little, as they wished her to be quiet. By three o'clock the doctor knew it was pernicious malarial fever, of the worst form imaginable, and medicine had failed to do its work. At 6 a. m. on Tuesday she said to the missionaries that, unless a change for better came soon, she would not be with them long. All work was stopped and all was done that could be done for her. After 8 a. m. she was delirious and called Miss Groenendyke, 'Jennie' (the name of her stepsister). In the afternoon the missionaries, with George Keister and Thomas Hallowell, gathered in the doctor's room, and prayed for her. They felt comforted and took it to mean her recovery, but it was only strength for the terrible blow that was to follow. At 8 p. m. on Tuesday, July 19, 1892, after a few tossings in her bed, she quietly passed away, to be 'forever with the Lord.' As we knelt around the bed we felt it was the Father's will. In her delirium she would say, 'I do not want to be out of employment,' and so it was 'only one day with nothing to do, and even then doing a great work on the hearts of all who saw her.'"

Miss Groenendyke wrote to her father, "I chose her prettiest clothing when we dressed her for the tomb, a pretty plaid lawn that had come in her box, with white ribbon for the waist and neck. The carpenters made her coffin and we covered it with white muslin and trimmed it with swiss. A crown of trailing ferns, dotted with white flowers gathered by the boys, decorated the lid. Her funeral was preached the next day at noon, in the chapel, by Brother Miller, from Heb. 13: 14, 'For here have we no continuing city, but we seek one to come.' The songs sung were, 'Home of the Soul,' 'Blessed Assurance,' and 'Sweet By-and-By.' She was buried near the chapel, and her grave filled by her Sabbath-school class and the boatmen with whom she was so well acquainted. Her age was thirty-two years, two months, and twenty days. Heaven is nearer and more real now to us since she is there. We think if she could have chosen a place to die it would have been just where it was. For if it was to her such a blessed place to live, it certainly would have been her wish to die among the people for whom she had lived."

What must have been her joy, when the next month Elma Bittle came from the same place to join her. They were dear friends, and among the last things was a conversation between the girls about Otterbein University, when the doctor said, "Girls, you must go to bed now," Frankie started away laughing, and said, "When we get to heaven we will talk all we want to about the dear old place." Two months later, from Shaingay, Brother Gomer, whom she loved, came to the heavenly company, and two years afterwards Brother West, whose ideal missionary, Christian worker, and in fact everything, she was, and he who once shouted as together they sang,

> "Then sweeping up to glory, to see His blessed face,
>   Where rivers of delight shall ever roll,"

as they were going from the river up to the mission house.

And now, nearly six years later, from the same field, and in sight of the same place, comes her dear Doctor Hatfield and Miss Schenck, who watched with her all of the last night of her earth life, with their martyrs' crowns upon their heads. And the other five whom she never knew here, but to whom she needed no introduction there.

To us this young life ended all too soon, but to Him who measures our lives by deeds, not years, it was enough, and she was called "up higher." But as she had not lived in vain, so her death was not in vain, and as this imperfect sketch of her life is given to the public, may a double portion of her cheerfulness, her happiness, and her willingness to be used in "joyful service for her King" be the inheritance of every reader, for his name's sake.

> " Oh, how sweet it will be in that beautiful land,
>   So free from all sorrow and pain,
>   With songs on our lips, and with harps in our hands,
>   To meet one another again."

Elma Bittle.
BY MARY BITTLE.

On November 18, 1863, Elma Bittle came to gladden the home of George and Martha Bittle, near Lewisburg, Ohio. While a mere child she became her father's constant companion. Many acres of land were plowed, the father holding the plow and the child the plow-line. She became extremely fond of nature and early evinced a strong affection for all dumb animals, her first playmate being her dog, Rover.

When very young she learned to read, and her few books made deep impressions on her mind. One of her teachers has said, "No reprimands were given her, for she always prepared her lessons as one much older than she would prepare them." She loved the poets, Whittier being one of her favorites. She pored over "Uncle Tom's Cabin" until she knew it from cover to cover, this book making a lasting impression upon her young mind, and doubtless first turned her thoughts toward Africa. One of Whittier's poems, "A Sabbath Scene," also influenced her, that poem being the only committed article she was willing to give in public, as she always disliked public speaking.

She loved to please and instruct, and at the age of seventeen she taught her first school. Moved by her determination to be equal to her ideal of the true teacher, she spared no pains nor efforts to attain excellence in her vocation. In September, 1884, she began teaching in the intermediate room of the Lewisburg school. Prayerfully and earnestly she filled this place for four years, at the expiration of which she yielded to a strong desire

to attend college, and better fit herself for her life-
work.

From 1888 to the fall of 1890 she attended
Otterbein University, where under the leadership
of the noted Robert E. Speer, she offered herself
to the volunteer band. When yet a child she expressed her desire to be a missionary, India being
her chosen field. She desired to especially fit herself for foreign work.

She was elected in the fall of 1890 to go to West
Elkton, Preble County, Ohio, as primary teacher in
the graded school. So forcible were her impressions to follow at once the call of her Master that
she resigned her position at this place and entered
the Master's vineyard in a foreign land.

The oldest child of the family, she was ever the
counselor and the inspiration of her younger
brothers and sisters, their true, brave leader.

"I gave My life for thee,
What hast thou given for me?"

She enlisted while a delegate to the Woman's
Missionary Board, which convened at Decatur,
Illinois. From Decatur she wrote her sister Mary
thus: "While I feel that I should like to better prepare myself for foreign work, I know this is an
opportunity, and I must go." A few days after her
decision, she was offered a position as teacher in
the Industrial School for Boys, at Lancaster,
Ohio, but this was pushed aside, for her duty she
felt lay in foreign fields.

Seeing that her soul was in the going, her people
said no word of discouragement to her, and cheerfully prepared for her departure, which occurred

Miss Elma Buttle.

at half past seven o'clock on the morning of September 8, 1891.

A sojourn of two weeks through the east was planned for, and at every resting-place a letter of good cheer was received by the family from Elma. She wrote, "Try to be glad and happy." She gave a graphic description of the route to New York City and a long letter describing that city. From the vessel she writes:

"Steamship, *City of Chicago,*
"September 23, 1891.

"Dear Folks:—

"We are off at last and are now rounding Sandy Hook. The pilot soon leaves us to ourselves, and then we shall be altogether cut loose from American shores. The land will soon fade from view, and yet I am not in the least homesick or sad. We shall be separated by a few miles only.

"The water looks lovely and I feel well so far— only about an hour out of the harbor as yet. Wonder how I shall feel to-morrow by this time? Will keep you informed as to my condition. We have met Miss Benedict and like her.

"Good-by, with love,
"Elma."

A letter was written on board the vessel and mailed from Queenstown; another was written in Liverpool, describing life as she saw it there, and also containing a complete description of Chester, England. A long letter was received from Madeira Islands, and another when the final landing was made at Freetown.

Extract from letter, November 9, 1891:

"ROTUFUNK, WEST AFRICA.

"Last night I had just got settled in my bed, when I heard a slight rustling under my pillow, I listened and heard it again, more distinctly by that time. I concluded to arise hastily and investigate. Upon lighting my lamp I found a lizard's slender appendage protruding from between my pillows. I soon got quite out of bed and called to Mrs. Miller, asking what I should do to get rid of it. She came up armed with an umbrella and tried to kill it, but it ran under a box and got away. Now I carefully examine my bed, for the harmless little creatures are not quite as innocent looking to me as they will be by and by. A piece of coal that I have is a great curiosity to the boys; each one of them takes it up and smells of it almost the first thing. My long hair also surprises them, the women, especially.

"For the past two Sundays we have had 110 and 111 respectively at Sunday school, and that with all the rest gone. We always go out to invite the people in. I enjoy it very much. One woman whom I invited so many times and who did not come, I told yesterday I would not ask her to come, that she did not tell me 'true word' when I did ask her, so I would not say anything more to her. To my surprise she came to Sunday school. A certain man had promised me over and over to come, and failed to do so, so when he said yesterday he would come, one of the boys who was along said his eyes said he would not come, but he did, and he was at prayers, too, this morning.

"These people are not at all slow to learn, and they are slyer than any one I have had to do with at home. Once learn them, and you will not find it hard to control them and head them off.

"The people use the term 'mammy' as a term of respect, so I often receive that name. The boys say I 'get sharp eye,' and Jonathan says he 'no like how I can look,' and that I am able to see everything that goes on in the schoolroom without taking my eyes from my book. He says that 'Mammy sabba fos teach school, but please ma make you no look me,' they all hate to be 'looked with a bad eye.'

"We get on 'tip-top' at school and I think we are the best of friends, even if they do not fancy my 'looking.'

"Daddy Queen, of whom you read in the *Evangel*, works a great deal in our wood-house and at the well, so I see considerable of him. He has taught me some Mendi expressions, and you ought to see his old face light up when I say them to him. He says, 'You tell um plain.' I always say, 'How do' to him in Mendi.

"July 5. The rain is pattering down in good earnest. As it falls upon the tin roof of the west piazza it sounds like it used to when we lived in the old house, and the rain dripped down at the west door. I am as cosy as can be in my snug, tidy little room, with these memories of home about me. This year I won't hear the click of the mowers and reapers *for the first time in my life*. On the Fourth I wondered if you were not cutting the wheat.

"Mr. Miller is still in bed, but better. Baker is

better, but Miss Hatfield is down this morning with one hundred and two degrees. So it goes. I am not afraid of this fever any more."

This letter was received one week after the news of her death reached America—the last she wrote:

"Rotufunk, West Africa,
"July 22, 1892.

"My dear Folks:—

"I am only going to write you a short letter, since it is expected that we can send mail in a few weeks again, and there is so much writing to do to other parties between this and Monday, when the messenger goes. I expected to write to-day, but had taken some calomel, which usually 'lays one up' for a day, so I did not write until this evening. My throat has been in an irritated condition for a week or two, just as it has been so many times in my life. I am amused greatly at Mrs. Miller, who insists upon being alarmed at my horrid snoring. She is afraid I'll choke, and when I laugh she looks rather incredulous as though I hardly knew. Miss Hatfield is swabbing my throat and it is much better. I do not find it more troublesome here than at home. Aside from the little sore throat, which only hurts when I swallow, I am still quite well. This rainy weather is much more trying upon one, of course, than the dry season. Mr. Miller has had an attack of fever, so has Doctor Hatfield, in the last two weeks, but both are well again. They were not very bad, that is, it was not serious. I also had an elevation of one hundred and one and a half degrees last week, one night, but got up the next morning and went to work, apparently none the worse for it. I seem to recover more quickly than the others from fever. I believe I am over the notion of having the fever at all, for I am convinced that we are better for an attack now and then. Mr. Miller has had no fever since soon after Christmas, but see how affected he was for the greater part of the first year. Quinine is next to bread, the staff of life, for missionaries in Africa.

"We have decided, with the advice of the doctor, that ten to fifteen grains of quinine are necessary for us weekly. When I feel malaria I take quinine until my head 'buzzes,' then I stop until next time. I am afraid you will get tired of this old story, but I want you to know that I am conscientiously careful, and I shall even be more careful from this time on.

"I presume that the telegram which was sent the Board this week has already been given out to the people, and that you already know that our number has been lessened by death. Miss Williams left us on last Tuesday evening at eight o'clock, the first United Brethren missionary to go to heaven from Africa.

"We have had a hard stroke, such as you can only partly understand from across the water. One year ago such a sorrow would almost have crushed me, but my coming to, and my stay in, Africa has taught me such lessons that to-day I can 'sing above the battle strife.' I think this is the hardest stroke of my life, even leaving you all as I did last year was not like this; you were all alive and there were hopes that we should meet again, but when you have once lived as we have here, a little community within ourselves, no other source upon which to draw for sympathy or direction in work, where one must be mind, heart, and conscience for the people with whom we labor, then you can understand what it is to have one of our little body die.

"Frankie had always been so well and so free from malarial disturbances that we all with her considered her health most remarkable. She was always so active and full of life, ready for every meeting, and did so much work. She was superintendent since November last, and had a greater responsibility resting upon her than any one realized until now. The boys were her care also, and thirty-two African boys to manage and plan for, means more than you can ever know in America. She was always the same happy, cheerful, hopeful person at all times.

"We were together a great deal, and talked very confidentially to each other on many matters. It was a kind of standing joke among the missionaries that she and I never got through talking. One day when some one laughed at us, she said, 'Well, never mind; when we get to heaven we'll have time to finish our talk. Won't we talk then?'

"On Saturday afternoon I went over to talk with her, and stayed almost the entire afternoon. She read me a letter she had written to Mrs. Keister and together we corrected it. On Sunday we stayed at the chapel between the church service and Sunday school. In the evening I went over to stay with Baker, who was not yet well enough to go out to church, and I was surprised to see Miss Williams at home. At the dinner table she and

Mrs. Vercoe, with Doctor Hatfield, had gotten into a discussion over me—an old joke it was—and when I appeared on the scene they started up again. We all laughed very heartily over the foolish remarks that were exchanged among us, then separated. The mail came the same evening with our letters.

"On Monday morning, while I was making my bed, I saw Miss Williams coming over to our house, running part of the way, and singing, as she usually did. I heard her come into the house, speak a few words to Mr. Miller, and before I knew it she was at the head of the stairs calling out to me in her cheery tones. She sat down near me and we talked quite a while; then together we went down-stairs, where she read several letters to Mrs. Miller. I left the room, and when I came back she was gone, but I went out on the piazza and hollowed good-by after her. She said I must remember this was the evening to talk, and laughed.

"In the evening after I came home from school the girls said that Miss Hatfield told them Miss Williams could not go to Young People's Christian Endeavor meeting; that meeting we managed together. On the way to the meeting Miss Schenck called to me, as we passed the mission-house, and said, 'Do you know Miss Williams is sick?' I said, 'Yes; I wonder if I had better come in to see her?' She said she hardly thought the doctor would agree to let me in. I knew both of us would want to talk too much and so passed on. After the meeting I stopped again, hoping to see her, but Doctor Hatfield said I had better not go in for she was pretty sick. But I forgot to tell you she had been at work all day on Monday, and did not want to go to bed even when she did. Doctor Hatfield saw that she looked bad when she came home from school, and asked her if she felt well; she said she was tired only, and did not think she had fever. Miss Hatfield found her pulse very fast, and upon taking her temperature found it above one hundred and three degrees. She begged to be allowed to stay up until after dinner, but the doctor said 'No; she must not.'

"Very reluctantly she went to bed, but in a short time she grew sick indeed. On Tuesday morning early I had to go to the schoolhouse, and again I stopped to inquire about her. Miss Groenendyke said, 'Well, she is the sickest person we have had in this mission for two years, except Mrs. Miller. She vomited all night long and cannot retain any medicine, either by taking it into the stomach or by injection Nothing seems to affect her.'

"About nine o'clock Miss Groenendyke sent me a note, saying there could be no school, and that I must get ready for the night watch, also that from the human standpoint there was but little hope. I went over to inquire further and found them all in tears, but trying to work against hope. Miss Hatfield said, 'She looks death-stricken; her pulse is 140, and everything I can do seems to be of no avail. But I shall try as long and as hard as I can. Oh, this is hard!'

"I could do nothing but go home and get ready for the night. You can imagine with what a sore and heavy heart I went. About 2 P. M. Miss Groenendyke telephoned for us to come. We found her much worse and almost wholly unconscious. Occasionally she opened her eyes and said a word or two, but I do not think she recognized any of us. Two or three times I succeeded in getting her to open her mouth to take medicine, by calling her by her first name—we always addressed each other thus when talking alone. Two, and part of the time three, were needed to keep her covered and in bed. Her vomiting ceased and she retained the medicine by injections. But the 'black vomit' had appeared. The doctor watched her while the remaining ones, with Thomas Hallowell and George Keister, gathered in a little prayer-meeting to pray the Lord to spare her if it were his will.

"We all felt so relieved after that, and while I interpreted my feelings to mean that she would recover, yet I was not certain, but I felt that if the worst came I was better able to bear it.

"Miss Groenendyke and I watched with her the greater part of the time after 2 P. M., although the doctor and Miss Schenck were in and out assisting and taking turns with us, the doctor especially, being the anxious, careful, never-tiring watcher.

"Miss Williams' fever was the pernicious type of malarial fever, often mistaken for yellow fever, and while the matter vomited was black, yet it was not the real black vomit of yellow fever.

"Sometime after 7 P. M. Mr. Miller came in and said to me, 'You had better go and rest awhile and let me watch.' I went into Miss Hatfield's room and threw myself upon the bed. Soon she came in, and we lay talking in the dark. When she left me to go and take Frankie's temperature, I turned over, thinking to sleep a little. I was just dozing when Miss Hatfield called, 'Miss Bittle, you 'd better come.' In a moment I was in the room where the sufferer lay. A few long breaths, a few gasps, and only the tenement of clay was left to us.

"As I looked I thought, 'This is the end of earth.' 'My ways are not your ways,' for we would not have had it so.

"There were quite a number in the room. Mr. Miller and Miss Groenendyke thought it could not be that she was gone. Doctor Hatfield, with a heart full of aching and grief, went from one to the other, comforting and consoling. I could not cry. My heart seemed turned to stone, yet our grief was very quiet, as it was under control, for here were mission children and outside people to look after.

"Soon a large company of people gathered upon the piazza and had we made any loud manifestations, there would have been an awful outcry, for when any one dies here there is loud wailing, tearing of hair, etc. Baker said yesterday that one of the old women said, 'Now, if this were in the country land—native custom—they would be crying loud, but the English never cry loud.' Two of the old women, her especial charges, came up to me and took hold of my hands, weeping and sympathizing. It has been a bitter, bitter stroke to the boys.

"Miss Groenendyke and I, by request, washed and dressed her, and by ten o'clock she lay peaceful and quiet on the lounge in the parlor. She was in bed only twenty-eight hours. There were no dying words to remember, but what does that matter when her life was so full of good words and cheerful acts. I tell you I do not think of death as I once did. It is not so terrible any more, and I am more and more convinced that it matters only what our living is like, and that we ought to live each day as though it is to be our last, for just see how quickly Miss Williams was gone. One morning she was here; the next evening she lay asleep in the mission-house parlor.

"Do you know that Frankie's death here was the first one I had seen since Brother Frankie's, when I was a child? Strange that it should be in Africa, and also that my first experience in preparing a body for burial should be in a foreign land.

"But deep as our sorrow is, the comfort from God is just as deep. There is such a peaceful resignation, such a drawing near to our Lord that we cannot weep much. Heaven seems much nearer and more real as our abiding place. It is a bitter experience, but I cannot make you understand how much it has already added to my life. I feel so humbled by it.

"That same night the carpenters were put to work upon the coffin. In the morning, as soon as the coffin was finished, Mrs. Miller and Miss Groenendyke covered it neatly with white muslin. making a neat pillow and cushion about the head and face. Miss Schenck and I covered the lid. I thought, while we were working, how strange it would seem to do such things in America, and yet we found comfort in doing it, since it seemed necessary. At twelve we went to the chapel, where the services were held. Mrs. Thompson and Miss

Florence and Mr. Johnson were here, too. It was with aching hearts, broken voices, and eyes much of the time filled with tears, that we sang and Mr. Miller preached. The Christian's way of mourning in America often partakes of the heathen custom greatly, as I now can see, and we wanted to make the people know that, while we were sad, yet our hearts were fixed on Him who doeth all things well. I am glad God never makes a mistake. Had we been consulted we'd have said that any one else could be better spared from the work than Frankie Williams. But how little we know. The work remains and she is gone.

"The chapel was filled—a beautiful tribute to her life among the people, for she was well beloved. Old Mammy Parks said, 'Mampeow, ya' (good-by, lady). Another said, as they do to each other when going on a journey, 'Walk good, oh.'

"She was carefully and tenderly laid away in the chapel yard, by the side of Mr. Helmick, who died about two years ago, the first white missionary to find a resting-place in the United Brethren missions of west Africa.

"We shall have to double up until the Wests return. I am to go to the other house now to assist there, and in my next letter can tell you how my work has been changed. Miss Groenendyke is now at the head of the mission. While our hearts are sad, yet we are happy.

"Two or three times I wished I could slip into the sitting-room for a few minutes to talk over things with you all, but that is gone now and we are ourselves again. Even sorrow can hallow most sweetly.

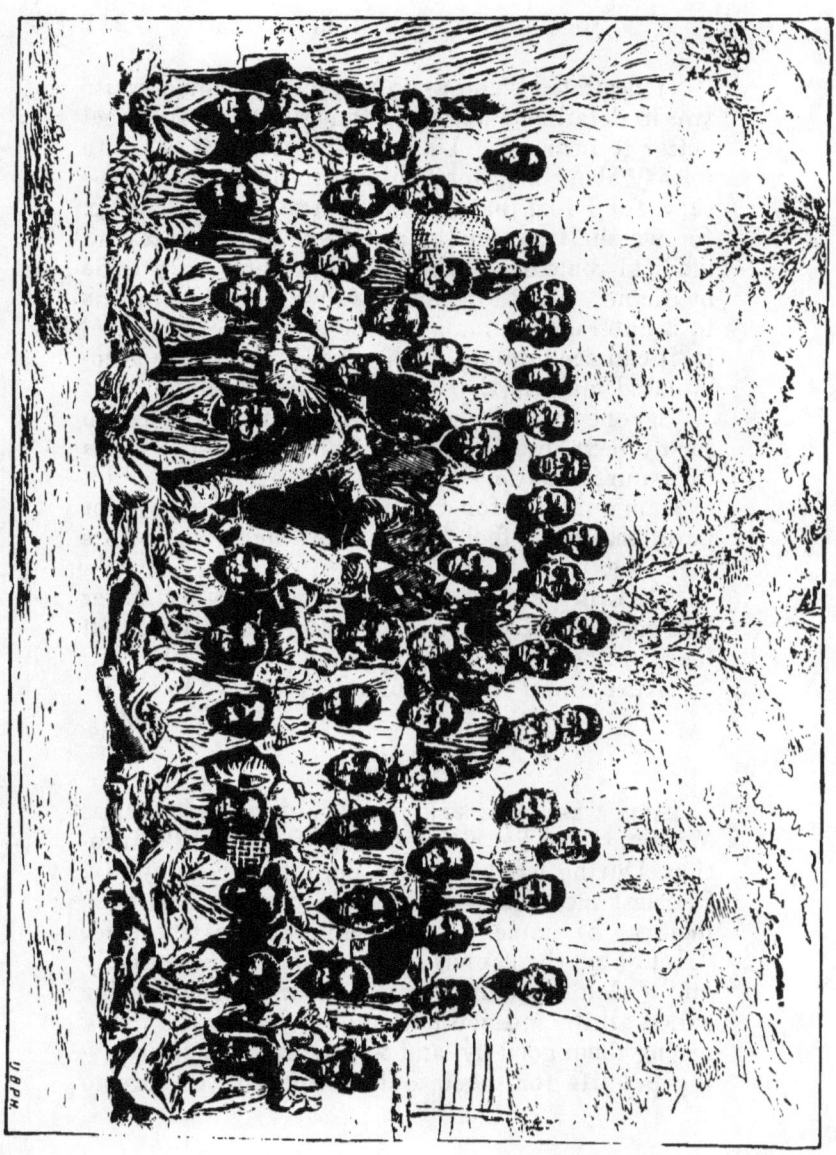

SHANGAY SCHOOLBOYS.

"I hesitated some as to whether I should write you in detail as I do, but I thought you would feel better to hear all. I am afraid you will be more uneasy about me, but I do not think that is necessary, for I feel that we are even safer than before, for we shall pay closer attention to ailments and medical remedies. Frankie took very, very little medicine. Miss Hatfield says we need the quinine to counteract the malaria, for even before we feel it, it can accumulate. She thinks it was the accumulated malaria that carried away Frankie.

"I hope to have more cheerful news to give you in my next letter. This is only one of the trials in a missionary's life; but after all I would not exchange my lot for any other. I am far happier here, because I feel that this is where God wants me to be.

"Give my love to everybody. Your last letter was good, and I was so glad and proud of Hal, that tears of joy came in my rejoicing.

"Next time I'll say more. Love, love to all.
"ELMA."

LAST HOURS.

Elma was taken sick just two weeks after Miss Williams, and her sickness was of one week's duration. During her last hours she talked continually. She left messages for her family and called each member by name. To the missionaries she said, "Hold high the banner of Jesus and bear it bravely on," "God's promises are just and true." She called all the mission boys and girls into the room, giving them good-by, and telling them she was giving her life for them, and for them to be sure to live pure, Christian lives. She asked Mr. Miller to preach her funeral sermon from the text, "Watch and pray," and begged him to tell the people at Rotufunk what it cost to bring them the gospel of light and liberty.

Thursday, at 10:30 P. M., August 7, 1892, in a far-away heathen land, Elma entered into the joy of the Lord. She died, as she had lived, for others.

> "Alike is life and death,
> When life in death survives,
> And the uninterrupted breath
> Inspires a thousand lives."
> —*Longfellow.*

The Funeral.

On the morning of the 8th of August, 1892, the little band of sorrowing missionaries laid away all that was left of their comrade, Elma Bittle. They placed her in the plain wooden muslin-covered casket, while on the lid was placed a wreath of ferns and frangipani, and bore her to the chapel. Although the rain came down in torrents, the little chapel was filled with sympathizing friends. Mr. Miller conducted the services, assisted by Rev. J. B. Johnson, of Palli. With trembling heart and tear-dimmed eyes Mr. Miller preached from the text which Elma had chosen, Matt. 26: 41, "Watch and pray."

He preached as one inspired, and his words made a profound impression upon the hearts of those who listened. After the services Elma was borne by her boys (her request) to the little God's acre back of the chapel, and laid beside her dear friend Frankie.

In the hope of the resurrection she rests.

From one of the mission boys to Seymour Bittle:

"Rotufunk Station, West Africa,
"August 31, 1892.

"My dear Seymour:—

"I am very glad to write this letter. Since I have written to you I never received any answer from you, but I did not feel bad about it, for I know that your heart is troubled and I know a little how your feelings are in your heart. Now I am going to explain as far as I know. One Sunday afternoon two of us went to see Miss Bittle. When we went she talk to us good, and she was well and strong, and when we were talking Doctor Hatfield came in and we have good time. Then Miss Bittle said, 'When I die I shall want my boys to bear my coffin.' Then we laugh at it. Then on the next morning she was strong and she works. In the evening time, about three o'clock, she have a fever, and one of the young men ask her if she is sick. She says 'No,' in a low tone. She says, 'I am resting only.' Then on the other day she was sick and the doctor did not allow us to go inside the room. Then on Thursday night she was better, then on Friday night the sick was strong again, and the doctor try her best to help her. Then on Saturday she sent some one to call us, and when we went she bade us good-by, but the doctor said she will not die yet. On Sunday night the doctor said that she will die in a few hours more. When she want to die she call us together and bade us good-by. When I entered in the room she call me and said, 'My dear boy, remember the words that I tell you,' and she die. When she die three of us sit in the room by her until morning. Now I close.

"From your friend,
"BAKER WYANDT."

From one of the young mission girls to Bessie Bittle:

"ROTUFUNK, WEST AFRICA,
"December 2, 1892.

"My dear Bessie:—

"I am very glad to write you these few lines. I wanted to write you for a long time after the death of your sister. We love her very much. We can't express how much we love her, but we love her with all our hearts. But it is the Lord's wish to take her away from us. You don't know how we feel when she died, but we all hope to meet her in that world on high. I remember when I was talking with her I said if she is sick she must not go to school, but when she was yet in the Girls' Home, and asked me if I want another missionary to die. The next day she went over to the mission-house. We did not like to see her go, but we can't help it. When she went she got sick and died there. She died between ten and eleven o'clock. I did not sleep until daybreak. I was in my bed thinking what great sin I have done that the Lord put such heavy thing on me, but whatsoever the Lord sees best he will do it to us. I hope you well with your brother. Miss Bittle often told us about you, how you would play at home, how Seymour would leave his shoes and you would take them and clean them and then go after him with them. I often think of you. I do pray for you always. Don't feel too bad. If you are good, you meet her in heaven. Good night. My love to all friends.

"I am your sister in Christ Jesus.
                                    "LYDIA JARVIS."

"The dear Lord's best interpreters
   Are humble human souls,
The gospel of a life like hers
   Is more than books or scrolls.

"From scheme and creed the light goes out,
   The saintly fact remains,
The blessed Master none can doubt,
   Revealed in holy lives."
                                    — *Whittier.*

JOSEPH GOMER.
BY REV. WILLIAM M'KEE, D.D.

This faithful servant of God, and for twenty-two years a faithful missionary in Africa, was brought up on a farm near Battle Creek, Michigan. But little is known of his childhood or boyhood days. He learned to be industrious, and got the rudiments of a common-school education in his native state; though at that time no colored children could attend a school, even in the free North, without being subjected to daily sneers and insults from the wiser and greater, so-called, and self-esteemed of the white children. On account of this tabooing practice so often indulged in by the scholars, and not always discouraged, but rather winked at by teachers and school trustees, Joseph attended rather irregularly only a few terms of the country school. However, he learned to read and write, and got a smattering of arithmetic, English grammar, and geography. But this foundation, slender and insufficient as it was, proved a mine of wealth to him in after years.

The next thing known definitely of Joseph Gomer is that he is a soldier wearing the United States' uniform, and sworn to support the flag and suppress the Great Rebellion, which to him meant not only the destruction of the so-called confederacy, but the freeing of three and a half million of slaves, whose only crime was that they were black. As a soldier he did his duty and did it well, patiently, bravely, loyally.

The War over, Mr. Gomer started home on a steamer from New Orleans, and soon found, among other passengers, an attractive widow lady and her daughter, whose home was at Chillicothe, Ohio. The daughter was sixteen or eighteen years of age.

Before they reached Cincinnati they became quite well acquainted. Finally Mr. Gomer began to talk matrimony to the widow. This astonished her. She supposed, possibly, he might want her daughter, but that he should want the mother had not entered her mind. However, on landing at Cincinnati they came at once to Dayton, where in the Third United Brethren Church Mrs. Green became Mrs. Gomer. Rev. J. D. Bottles, of Miami Conference, officiated at the marriage. This was in 1865. Mr. Gomer soon found profitable employment in a large mercantile house, as foreman of the department for measuring, making, and fitting of carpets. In the church he was always in the position of leader, steward, trustee, or superintendent of Sunday school, sometimes filling two or three positions at once, and he was always the same faithful, earnest, reliable man in the church that he was in his business relations. He believed in, and practiced serving the Lord in the street, and in all the business affairs of life as well as in the church.

In 1871 the Parent Board found itself in straitened conditions for laborers in the African field. Mr. and Mrs. Hadley returned to America early in April, 1869, and on the twenty-eighth day of that month Mr. Hadley had gone to his eternal reward.

Mr. J. A. Williams, who had long served in the capacity of assistant, when an American was there, and as sole manager when alone, had died September 2, 1870. He died in faith, and peace, and blessed hope. This left the mission with none but a few native helpers, and they not well qualified for the work. New missionaries were hard to find. At this juncture it was remembered that Mr. Gomer had been heard to say that he would be glad to go to Africa as a missionary, if he were qualified for the task. So, after casting about a little, as Samuel did for a king, and not finding what it wanted elsewhere, the Board turned to Mr. and Mrs. Gomer, with the question, "Will you go as missionaries to Africa?" Soon they answered, "Yes; if you can use us to any advantage at all." Accordingly, the executive committee, on the eighth of November, 1870, appointed Mr. and Mrs. J. Gomer to take charge of our mission work in Africa; and on the tenth of December, 1870, they sailed from New York, arriving in Freetown, West Africa, January 11, 1871.

ARRIVED IN AFRICA.

To show what we had in Africa when Mr. Gomer reached the field of his future labors, I give one of the last, perhaps the last letter, Mr. Hadley wrote from Africa to the corresponding secretary:

"Our day-school is not what we desire it to be, nor what it ought to be. We have only about twenty scholars. Our Sabbath school has been more interesting. This is due principally to the distribution of reward tickets and books for memorizing scripture. We have one officer, three teachers, and twenty-four scholars, and 5,132 verses of scripture have been memorized and repeated. Six of our best scholars have repeated 3,575 of these. Our prayer-meetings and Tuesday evening Bible class have been very good. Five persons whom we had greatly hoped to see converted soon, are, for the present, apparently out of our reach; but another one has lately given evidence of distress on account of sin." This was what we had after fourteen years of effort!

However, when Mr. Gomer arrived he was received with great deference by Mr. Caulker, the chief, and by the people generally. He won their confidence at once. The chief had never before allowed his slaves, or anybody else, if he could help it, to attend the Sabbath school, the Bible class, or the preaching service. But on June 15, 1871, Mr. Gomer wrote: "We feel very much encouraged. All our meetings are well attended. At the barra (court-house) great numbers stand outside. We had prayer- and speaking-meeting Sunday night at the barra, with palm-oil for lights. Old Mr. Caulker, the chief, himself spoke to the people, and urged them to become Christians. He said he prayed to God, and that God has blessed him, and that he knew that religion was good."

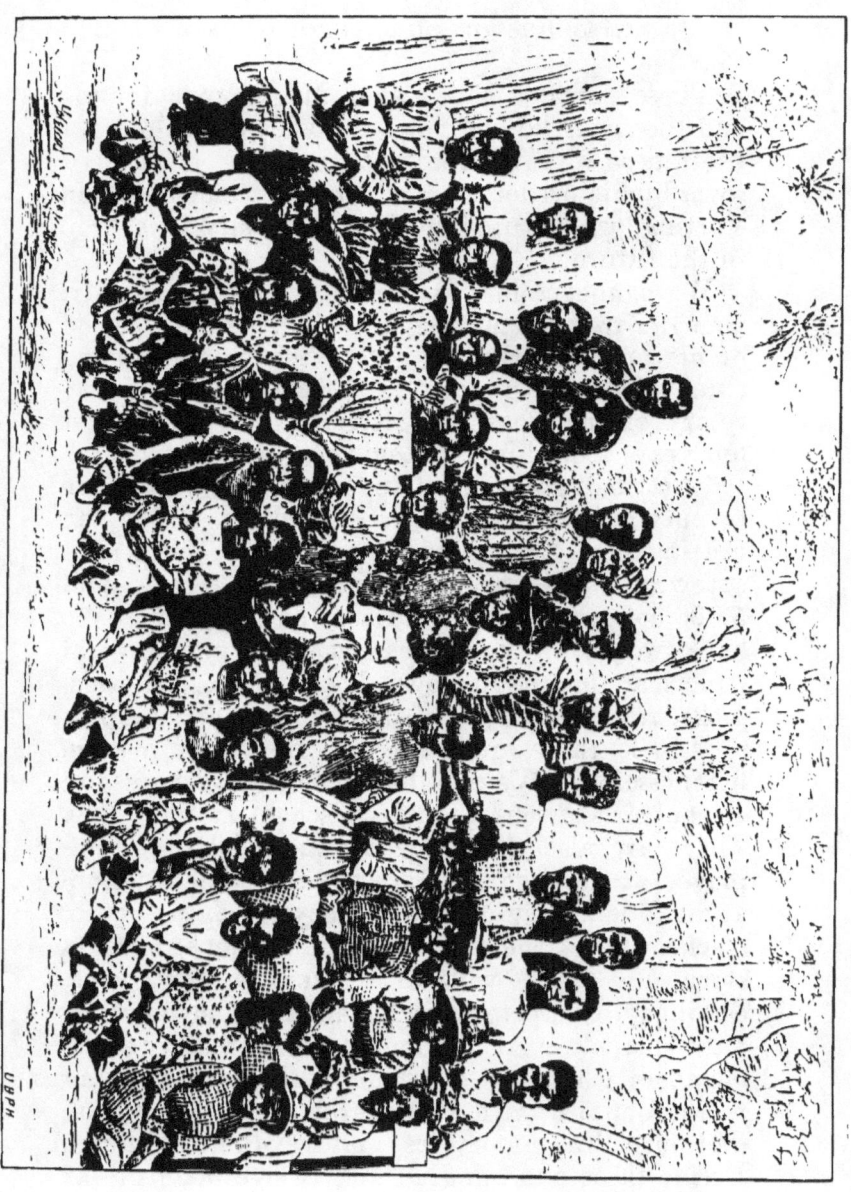
SHAINGAY SCHOOLGIRLS.

These extracts show what Mr. Gomer found; and the favor he met; and the wide-open door for usefulness revealed the fact that the good seed sown by his predecessors, though it seemed slow in starting, was springing up and promising a crop in the future.

We cannot follow in detail the path of Mr. Gomer's travels and labors during the long period of his service. But we give a few items gleaned chiefly from his reports to the corresponding secretary of the Board of Missions. In 1881, just ten years from his first beginning, he reported:

"At Shaingay, our principal station, we have seventy-five acres of cleared land, of which ten are in corn, twenty-three in cassava, and six in arrowroot. There are forty-four cocoa-trees, and 5,000 coffee-trees in the nursery on the farm. We have two oxen, five sheep, and seven pigs, several American plows, harrows, hoes, spades, shovels, picks, rakes, a supply of blacksmith's and carpenter's tools, three row-boats, six canoes, and a large fishing-seine. We now have twenty-five boys and eleven girls in our industrial school at Shaingay. There are also thirty-one common laborers employed at Shaingay. Here are the stone missionary residence, stone chapel, boys' lodging-house, blacksmith, carpenter, and tailor shops, mission store, and three wells of water. In the towns, Shaingay, Bompetook, and Mambo we have native-built chapels. At Shaingay we have fifty-seven members whom we can truly call such, and ten more to unite with the church. At Bompetook there are thirty members, and at Mambo fifteen. Beside these one hundred and twelve members of the church there are in the seekers' classes in different places one hundred and sixty-four. Many more would be with us if they were not slaves, and could carry out their own wishes. The whole country asks beseechingly for the gospel. Yandoo, Rembee, and Barcoh are especially solicitous to have schools and preaching. We must go ahead, and cannot wait for Sunday schools (in America) to come to our assistance. The gold and the silver are the Lord's, and in future my appeals shall be to him. Churches often disappoint us, but God never, when we go to him aright." These extracts reveal not only the work Mr. Gomer was doing under God, but also the spirit and character of the man. He was full of faith and good works.

To show what influence the gospel was exacting under the faithful administration of Mr. Gomer, I give another extract from a letter written March 14, 1881:

"Yesterday we received five new members into the church at Shaingay, three men and two boys. We should have taken four other men had they not been out of town. These men are old settlers at Shaingay and are heads of families.

"Of the present condition of the work we have no reason to complain. The people behave themselves well. The Sabbath is well observed, not only in Shaingay and the stations where our schools are located, but up the rivers and in the interior villages. When I compare ten years ago with the present it does not seem like the same place. Then every farm had its 'medicine,' and every hut its 'devil-house,' its 'twin-house,' or its 'sabba-house.' This latter is where the spirits of the old people are supposed to dwell. Now there are many villages where not one of these is to be seen. 'Devil-houses' are very scarce, and only occasionally do we come across a 'twin-house.' The future of the Sherbro country never looked more hopeful than at present."

As illustrating and confirming his own statements Mr. Gomer related what a Wesleyan missionary, stationed a few score miles from Shaingay, had to say: "In holding a conversation with a heathen man (as I took him to be) on religious subjects, I questioned him thus, 'My friend, why don't we see you come to the chapel on Sundays?' In reply, he said, 'Do you think that the few people you have got attending your chapel are the only results of your labors at Ponto Novo? No! But let me tell you that you have over four thousand private Christians, both men and women, who have received the Christian religion secretly, and are no worshipers of heathen gods, but are praying only to the true God of the Christians. They have renounced idolatry in their hearts, and have placed their whole and entire confidence in God and their Saviour, Jesus Christ. You do not know, nor see them, and I, who am speaking to you now, am one, yet you do not see me at your church among your people. Sir, we all believe that your religion, I mean the Protestant religion, is a true and better religion than paganism or heathenism, Mohammedanism, and our sister worshipers of idols, the Roman Catholics.' "

It will thus be seen that Mr. Gomer not only understood, but to a great extent, and on wide-reaching lines, commanded the situation. His limited English had developed into a most practical and useful education.

Mr. Gomer's Death.

After serving his day in a most honorable life of service for his Master he was called suddenly from labor to reward. On the sixth of September, 1892, there came flashing through the sea, as from the finger of God,

"Joseph Gomer, Dead!"

Although we knew his health was declining, and expected his retirement from the superintendency of our African missions in a brief time, yet this announcement brought great astonishment and heart sorrow at first; but on further reflection and prayer it became a source of comfort and joy that one so long faithful and so eminently useful and successful in the holy cause of Christian missions had been called up higher, and was given his crown, which, no doubt, has many stars that will be his chief glory in his place about the great white throne.

It will be observed by comparing dates that Mr. Gomer's term of service in Africa measured twenty-two years from the time of his appointment. During these long years of service he visited America three times, tarrying only a few months at a time; and these intervals were spent in traveling about through the church, making many addresses, thus instructing the people and stimulating their zeal in the cause of missions. His "outings," as he called them, were, therefore, simply a change in place and manner of his work.

He was, from the first, thoroughly consecrated to the cause of missions. He counted not his life dear unto himself that he might win Christ, and on his way win souls to Christ; and he counted it a special honor to call those who seemed farthest away from Christ to come and be saved.

During his last visit to America he "set his house in order," so far as a man could, saying he did not expect he would ever again be able to visit America. "But," he added, "it is as near heaven from Africa as from America; and I want no higher honor than to die on the field of my long labors and be buried alongside of Tom Tucker." The reader will remember that Mr. Tucker was one of the first converts in Africa, and became a most faithful and efficient helper to our missionaries.

When the end came Mr. Gomer and wife had gone to Freetown to accompany Mr. and Mrs. Jacob Miller, of the Woman's Board, as they were about to sail for America, and to do some trading for the Shaingay Station. The day's work done, the evening prayers offered to God by the two families, they retired to rest; and in less than an hour Mr. Gomer was seized with apoplexy, and before medical help arrived, though delayed but a few minutes, the soul of the good man had gone to God.

Let me add a few words from others. At a farewell meeting in the Third United Brethren Church, on the going forth at the first of Mr. and Mrs. Gomer, in 1871, Doctor Thomas, pastor of the First Presbyterian Church, of Dayton, made some remarks. Among other things he said: "The Lord has highly honored this church. He has passed over all these high spires and fine churches and rich congregations, and come to this little church, and selected a man and woman and put upon them the highest possible honor, that of carrying the gospel to the heathen in Africa."

At the memorial services held at the General Conference, 1893, Rev. W. J. Shuey said: "There is one feature which Brother Gomer possessed which has not been mentioned here to-night. He was a statesman; he was a diplomatist. Before he ended his life in Africa he became the umpire of many a difficulty among the natives. He was a judge, not only in Israel, but among the tribes with which he was surrounded. They brought their 'palavers' to him and he had such a thorough insight into human nature, and was so skilled in comparing the character of one man with that of another that he settled many difficulties among the natives in Africa, and led them to a higher and better way, made society better all about him, and gave them a higher type of civil government. Indeed it is difficult to conceive what might have been brought forth through Brother Gomer had he been educated as we find white men about us educated. He was naturally a man of intellectual strength and power."

Mrs. Mary W. Gomer.

It may be added that Mrs. Gomer fully shared Mr. Gomer's devotion to the work of missions in Africa. She made for him a Christian home indeed; and that of itself was an object lesson of incomparable value to the heathen, where slavery, polygamy, concubinage, and other iniquities had always been practiced. Mrs. Gomer was a Christian woman of noble life and character. After Mr. Gomer's decease she lingered nearly two years; and though by reason of age and infirmity she was no longer able to do much effective work, her very life was a benediction to the people.

But in April, 1894, she bade a final adieu to Africa and sailed for America. Here she lingered for nearly two years, when December 1, 1896, the good Shepherd took her to the fold in heaven.

Mrs. Gomer was ill at ease in America. Her friends of a quarter of a century before had scattered abroad, and many of them had crossed the dark river. As the months wore away she thought and talked more of Africa, and the many and stirring incidents connected with her long labors among that people. She had so identified herself with them that they were her dearest friends in the world; and as the time for her departure drew nigh she talked of Mr. Gomer, of Shaingay, the schools, the churches, the boats, the ebbing and flowing tide, the boat rides in dark nights and on stormy seas. One evening she had unusual trouble (so it seemed in her delirium) in getting the boats, rowers, and other preparations ready for a trip across Youra Bay to Freetown. But before morning came the boat had landed her—in heaven.

They are not, for God has taken them.

APPENDIX.

Bishop Mills, Superintendent J. R. King, of the Sherbro-Mendi Mission, Superintendent L. A. McGrew and wife, and Miss Florence M. Cronise, of the Bompeh Mission, accompanied by thirty-six black men as porters, interpreters, guides, and cooks, in the month of December, 1896, made a journey through the Mendi country, going beyond Panguma, to Lalakun. Going eastward this party followed the path leading from Freetown through Rotufunk, Kwallu, Taiama, Mongherri, Gobabu, Jagbwima to Panguma. Returning, they parted company at Konduma, Bishop Mills and Mr. King and their men returning through Damballah, Jama, Mano, Jobahun Gbambaiah, Mano Bagru, to Bonthe. The other party returned through Taiama to Rotufunk.

The journey was undertaken to learn the proper places for locating new missions. Valuable information was obtained, and several new points have since been occupied, and other strategic points, it is hoped to enter soon. On this journey the following points of interest were given names:

1. Lucile Falls—A beautiful waterfall, about forty feet high, in the forest on the right side of the path going from Taiama to Mongherri, and three or four miles out of the latter city. It is the most lovely falls met on this journey.

2. Alfaretta Cascades, named in honor of the wife of Rev. J. R. King. They are a series of pretty falls in a stream on the left side of the path going from Mongherri to Gobabu, not far from the latter place.

3. Florence and Clara Peaks. These are lovely twin peaks on the left side of the path from Jagbwima to Dodo, and about three or four miles from the latter city. The one to the west is Florence; the other is Clara; named in honor of Florence M. Cronise and Clara B. McGrew.

4. Mount Mary (known to the natives as Mount Kuno), named in honor of the wife of Bishop Mills. It is on the right side of the path coming from Damballah to Jama, and is visible much of the way between these two cities.

Since no civilized names had been previously given to these objects, we hope that the English government will allow the names we have given them, for all time to come; and that our missionaries will hereafter call them by these names.

RULES FOR THE PRESERVATION OF HEALTH IN THE TROPICS.

(Taken from "Guide to Health in Africa," pp. 151-9, by Surgeon-Major T. H. Parke.)

Water.—All drinking water, no matter how sparkling and pure, should be invariably boiled, to insure its freedom from dangerous constituents. Cold weak tea, without sugar or milk, is best for the march. Water should always be drawn from up-stream, and from the center, if possible. Two grains of permanganate of potash to the quart, purifies water. If muddy, use alum.

Sun.—No precautions can be too great for protecting the head from the direct rays of the sun. The use of a proper head-dress and umbrella, also a spinal pad for morning and evening sun, is judicious.

Chills, draughts, sitting in damp clothes, especially when heated after violent exercise and copious perspiration, also cooling of the body suddenly in any way, are certain to be followed by fever.

Sleep as far as possible off the ground, and always under mosquito curtains at night.

Diet should be plain; meat, fish, vegetables, well-boiled fruit, rice, and cereals.

Alcohol during the day is most dangerous.

Tub in the early morning, or at the end of a march, before cooling; never while digestion is going on, and always tepid, if possible.

Camp.—Select highland plateau near water supply. Don't disturb the soil. Avoid ravines. Never to leeward of a swamp, unless separated by a belt of trees or a river. Site of latrine should be selected immediately on halting, and covered with a hurdle and sods so as to exclude flies, as they convey poison. Leave only a few openings, each about one foot square. Directly tent is pitched, hoe a gutter close to the walls.

Cleanliness.—Hair should be cut short.

Clothing.—The bodily temperature should be kept as equable as possible. Loosely-fitting woolen clothes are preferable. Light kamarband should be worn day and night. On halting after a march, put on a wrapper so as to cool gradually. Get under cover, and change, if possible.

[*Red Pepper.*—Eat plentifully with food, as a preventive of malarial fever.]

BOOKS OF REFERENCE.

On Africa in General.—"Africa," two volumes, Keane. "Actual Africa," Vincent. "The Partition of Africa," Keltie. "The Geography of Africa," Heawood. "In Darkest Africa," Stanley. "Tropical Africa," Drummond.

On Sierra Leone.—"Sierra Leone After One Hundred Years," Ingham. "Travels in West Africa," Kingsley. "Sketches of the Forestry in West Africa," Moloney. "A Lone Woman in Africa," McAllister.

On Our Missions in Sierra Leone.—"Thompson in Africa." "Sherbro Mission, West Africa," McKee. "Our Missionary Work," Flickinger.

The Best Small Work on Africa.—"Africa Waiting," Thornton.

MISSIONARIES SENT TO AFRICA BY PARENT BOARD.

W. J. Shuey—January 5, 1855, to June 15, 1855.

Daniel Kumler—January 5, 1855, to June 15, 1855.

D. K. Flickinger—January 5, 1855, to May 1, 1857; December 1, 1861, to April 15, 1862.

W. B. Witt—December 3, 1856, to June 25, 1858.

APPENDIX

J. K. Billheimer—December 1, 1856, to February 19, 1858; February 1, 1861, to May 1, 1864.

Mrs. J. K. Billheimer—February 1, 1861, to May 1, 1864.

C. O. Wilson—April 25, 1860, to August 11, 1861.

O. Hadley—October 22, 1866, to April 15, 1869.

Mrs. A. Mahala Hadley—October 22, 1866, to April 15, 1869; October 25, 1871, to June 22, 1874.

Joseph Gomer—November 8, 1870, to November 1, 1875; November 1, 1876, to April 1, 1889; November 15, 1889, died September 6, 1892.

Mary Gomer—November 8, 1870, to November 1, 1875; November 1, 1876, to April 1, 1889; November 15, 1889, to May 1, 1894.

J. A. Evans—October 25, 1871, to August 15, 1873; April 15, 1875, still in field.

Mrs. J. A. Evans—April 15, 1875, still in field.

Peter Warner—October 19, 1872, to July 20, 1874.

Mrs. Peter Warner—October 19, 1872, to April 30, 1873.

Joseph Wolf—November 14, 1874, to March 1, 1878.

Miss Lizzie Bowman—November 15, 1876, to December 10, 1877.

Daniel F. Wilberforce—November 6, 1878, to May 1, 1885; September 18, 1886, still in field.

Mrs. Lizzie Wilberforce—November 6, 1878, to May 1, 1885; September 18, 1886, still in field.

J. M. Lesher—October 6, 1883, to July 9, 1885; September 18, 1886, to May 1, 1887.

Mrs. J. M. Lesher—October 6, 1883, to July 9, 1885.

W. S. Sage—October 6, 1883, to December 4, 1885.

Mrs. W. S. Sage—October 6, 1883, to December 4, 1885.

L. O. Burtner—October 3, 1892, to April 1, 1896; October 1, 1897, to June 1, 1898.

Mrs. L. O. Burtner—October 3, 1892, to April 1, 1896; October 1, 1897, to June 1, 1898.

A. T. Howard—November 28, 1894, to May 1, 1898.

Mrs. A. T. Howard—November 28, 1894, to May 1, 1898.

J. R. King—November 28, 1894, to February 1, 1898; October 1, 1898.

Mrs. J. R. King—November 28, 1894, to February 1, 1898; October 1, 1898.

F. S. Minshall—October 17, 1896, to June 1, 1898.

Mrs. F. S. Minshall—October 17, 1896, to June 1, 1898.

WOMAN'S MISSIONARY ASSOCIATION.

TERM OF SERVICE OF MISSIONARIES IN AFRICA.

Miss Emily Beeken—Autumn, 1877, nineteen months.

Mrs. Mary M. Mair—October 19, 1879, to spring, 1883.

Rev. Richard N. West—October 2, 1882, to February 4, 1886; September 18, 1886, to March

31, 1891; October 1, 1892, died in Africa, September 26, 1894.

Mrs. Lida M. West—October 2, 1882, to February 4, 1886; September 18, 1886, to March 31, 1891; October 1, 1892, to January 19, 1895.

Rev. W. Sanford Sage—September 24, 1887, to October, 1890.

Mrs. Esther B. Sage—September 24, 1887, to October, 1890.

Miss Frances Williams—October 16, 1889, died in Africa, July 19, 1892.

Miss Ellen Groenendyke—October 16, 1889, to March 16, 1893.

Rev. Jacob Miller—November, 1890, to October, 1892.

Mrs. Ella Miller—November, 1890, to October, 1892.

Doctor Marietta Hatfield—September 23 1891, to October 29, 1895; October 1, 1897, massacred May 3, 1898.

Miss Elma Bittle—September 23, 1891, died in Africa, August 7, 1892.

Miss Ella Schenck—September 23, 1891, to January 19, 1895; October 1, 1897, massacred May 3, 1898.

Miss Lydia Thomas—October 1, 1892, to January 19, 1895.

Rev. Isaac Newton Cain—October 1, 1892, to June 6, 1896; October 1, 1897, massacred May 3, 1898.

Mrs. Mary Mutch Cain—October 1, 1892, to June 6, 1896; October 1, 1897, massacred May 3. 1898.

Miss Florence M. Cronise—November 28, 1894, to May 10, 1898.

Miss Minnie E. Eaton—November 28, 1894, to May 10, 1898.

Dr. Mary C. Archer—December 7, 1895, massacred May 3, 1898.

Rev. Lowry A. McGrew—March 28, 1896, massacred May 8, 1898.

Mrs. Clara B. McGrew—March 28, 1896, massacred May 8, 1898.

Mr. Arthur A. Ward—October 1, 1897, to May 5, 1898.

INDEX.

ADEN, GULF OF, 13.
Africa, location of, 13.
    size of, 13.
    relief, 14.
    white population of, 23.
    natives of, 24.
    six great curses of, 30.
African fever, 71.
Agulhas, Cape, 14.
Albert Edward, Lake, 15.
Albert, Lake, 15.
Alfaretta Cascades, 234.
Alligator Society, 69.
American Missionary Association, 73.
    work of turned over to United Brethren Church, 77.
    $300,000 expended by, 78.
Amharic language, 26.
Animals, 18, 40.
Ants, 18.
Appendix, 233.
Arabic, 26.
Archer, Dr. Mary, 127, 180, 240.
    life of, 150.
    letter of, 93.
Attack, Plan of, 123.
Avery, property at, 126.

BANGWEOLO, LAKE, 15.
Bantu, 24, 27.
Barra, a, 60, 224.

Beeken, Miss Emily, first Woman's Missionary Association missionary, 77, 238.
Berber, 25.
Berlin Conference, 19.
Bethany Cottage, 46, 161, 168.
Bible, 36.
Billheimer, J. K., 74, 78, 237.
Billheimer, Mrs. J. K., 237.
Bittle, Miss Elma, 156, 162, 201, 239.
    life of, 203.
    letters from, 208.
    last hours of, 217.
    funeral of, 218.
Blood, not on his hands, 143.
Bompeh District, 80.
    mission, 141, 183.
Bompetook, 225.
Bon, Cape, 13.
Bonthe, school at, 43.
    property at, 126.
Books of Reference, 236.
Bowman, Lizzie, 237.
Boys' home, 175, 192.
Brick, making of, 140.
British Central Africa, 20.
British East Africa, 20.
British rule beneficent, 67.
Brussels Conference, 33.
Bulloms, 47.
Bundoo, the, 68, 110, 175.
Burglars, 88.
Burning of mission buildings, 125.
Burtner, L. O., 121, 238.
Burtner, Mrs. L. O., 238.
Bushmen, 24, 27.

CAIN, REV. I. N., 127, 131, 138, 160, 171, 179, 180, 239.
    personal impressions of, 139.

Cain, Mary Elizabeth Mutch, 144, 239.
Canaries, 14.
Cannibalism, efforts to abolish, 121.
Caravans, 40.
Cardew, Frederick, 44, 92, 149.
Carrying trade, 39.
Caucasian type, 24.
Caulker, Lucy, 79.
Caulker, Thomas Neal, 79, 224.
Caulker, Thomas Stephen, 74.
Caulkers, history of, 75.
Chad, Lake, 16.
Childhood descriptive of native character, 53, 88.
Children, the, 99.
Christianity, 28.
Christians in Sierra Leone, 42.
Christians, private, number of, 227.
Church, the United Brethren, led to Sierra Leone, 115.
Civil service filled, 90.
Clark Training School, 43, 74, 102.
    library of, 104.
    course of study in, 104.
    results of, 105.
Climate, of Africa, 16.
    of Sierra Leone, 83.
    definition of, 51.
Clothing of natives, 57.
Coal a curiosity, 206.
Coffee trees, 225.
Colonial lines being drawn, 113.
Conference appointments of West Africa, 80.
Conference of missionaries in Sierra Leone, 45.
Configuration of surface, 51.
Congo Free State, 22.
Congo River, 15, 16.
Converts, 6,000, 79.
Country doctor, the, 95.

Criticism easy, 141.
Cronise, Miss Florence M., 105, 160, 240.
Curses of Africa, 30.
Customs of natives, 56.
  religious, 61.
  legal, 64.

DADDY Queen, 207.
Dances, of religious significance, 63.
Dancing, 70, 110.
  for dead, 175.
Dangers of the work, 86.
Dead, superstitions concerning the, 111.
Deaths of missionaries, few, 84.
Devil bush, 95.
Devil house, 62, 95, 226, 227.
Devils, 95, 110.
Diamonds, 19.
Difficulties of the work, 83, 86.
Drury, Prof. A. W., on import of the massacre, 128.

EATON, MINNIE, 102, 240.
Egypt, 20.
Egyptian, 25.
Empire, contention for, 117.
England, possessions of, 20.
Environment as affecting society, 51.
Ethiopian, 24.
Ethiopic, 25.
Evans, J. A., 237.
Evans, Mrs. J. A., 237.

FARMING of natives, 90.
Farms of General Board, 81.
Fauna, 18.
Feeble and deformed children, 69.
Fetish, the, 29, 62.

Fever, African, 83.
    how to avoid, 84.
Field, extent of the, 119.
Flickinger Chapel, 74.
Flickinger, D. K., 73, 78, 236.
Flora, 17, 41.
Florence and Clara Peaks, 234.
Folk-lore, 106.
Food, 60, 84.
Freedman's Mission Aid Society, 78.
    $13,000 given by, to United Brethren mission, 78.
Freetown, 37, 44.
    manner of life in, 39.
    a strategic point, 113.
French possessions, 19.
    population of, 113.
Fulah languages, 26.
Future, what of the, 128.

GENERAL BOARD, 223.
    possessions of, 81.
    expenditures of, 82.
    missionaries and terms of service, 236.
German possessions, 21.
Girls' Home, 163, 165, 172, 184, 192.
God, a supreme, 29, 61.
Gold, 19, 169.
Gomer, Joseph, 76, 78, 202, 237.
    life of, 221.
Gomer, Mrs. Mary W., 230, 237.
Groenendyke, Miss Ellen, 182, 190, 197, 201, 239.
Guardafui, Cape, 14.
Guilt, how determined, 65.
Guinea, gulf of, 16, 19.

HADLEY, O., 237.
Hadley, A. Mahala, 237.

Hamites, 24.
Hamitic family of languages, 25.
Hammock, only conveyance, 85.
Hatfield, Dr. Marietta, 127, 162, 174, 179, 202, 208, 239.
  life of, 153.
Health, preservation of, in tropics, 234.
Heroism, spirit of, not dead, 118.
Horses, not found in Sierra Leone, 84.
Hospitality of natives, 71.
Hott, Bishop, 157.
Hottentots, 27.
Houses of natives, 59.
Howard, Alfred T., 119, 238.
Howard, May S., 105, 238.
Hut tax, 122.

INDIAN OCEAN. 13, 15.
Industrial education needed, 92.
Industrial school, 225.
Ingham, G., quoted, 92.
Insects, 18.
Interpreters, difficulties with, 55, 107.
Italy, 22.

JARVIS, LYDIA, letter of, 220.
Jewish proselytes, 28.
Journey through Mendi country, 233.

KABYLE, 26.
Kaffir, 26.
Kephart, Bishop, 197.
King, J. R., 45, 160, 178, 238.
King, Mrs. Zella B., 85, 238.
Kroomen, the, 51.
Kumler, D. C., 73, 236.
Kuno, Mount, superstition concerning, 111.
Kurankoes, 48.

LANGUAGES, 25, 106.
    of Sierra Leone, 55.
Legal customs, 64.
Leicester, Mount, 46.
Leopard society, 69.
Leopold, Lake, 16.
Lesher, J. M., 237.
Lesher, Mrs. J. M., 238.
Limbas, 48.
Limpopo River, 16.
Livingstone on slavery, 34, 35.
Lizard as a bedfellow, 206.
Lokkohs, 47.
Lucile Falls, 233.
Lybian language, 25.

MADAGASCAR ISLAND, 14, 129.
Madeira Islands, 14.
Mair, Mrs. M. M., 77, 238.
Mambo, 225.
Mambo, not in existence, 50.
"Mammy," 207.
Mandingoes, 48.
Manufactures of natives, 91.
Massacre, the, 120.
Massacred, list of the, 137.
Mathews, George M., 168.
McGrew, Lowry A. and Clara B., 127, 160, 161, 179, 240.
    lives of, by W. L. Bunger, 166.
    lives of, by G. A. Funkhouser, D.D., 167.
    anecdote concerning, 169.
Medical treatment, 93, 156, 175.
Medicine men, 29.
Mediterranean Sea, 13.
Mendi, 49, 184, 185.
Mendi mission, 73.
Military road, 46.

Miller, Jacob, and Ella, 229, 239.
Miller, Mrs. L. K. 132, 159.
Minerals, 19.
Minshall, F. S., 43, 121, 238.
Minshall, Mrs. F. S., 238.
Missionaries, first ones, 73.
    number employed by Woman's Board, 77.
    inhospitable land for, 113.
    list of dead, 137.
    died in the faith, 138.
    tribute of Governor of Sierra Leone, 149.
Missionary conference, 45.
Mission boy, letter of, 219.
Mission girl, letter of, 220.
Mission work, 73.
    extent of United Brethren, 79.
    worthy of one's ambition, 117.
Mission work in Africa, 35.
Moero, Lake, 15.
Mohammedanism, 28, 31, 94, 114.
Mohammedan teachers, evil influence of, 90.
Money of natives, 70.
Mongherri, 169.
Morocco, 22.
Mount Mary, 111, 234.
Mozambique channel, 16.
Mullen, Miss, 160.
Music, 70.

NAMES of children, 58.
    adopted by natives, 76, 142.
Native Africans, 24.
Native-built chapels, 225.
Native teachers, why used, 114.
Need of aid, 119.
Negro languages, 26.
Niger River, 16.

INDEX

Nile River, 15, 16.
Noble band, 178.
Nuba languages, 26.
Nyassa, Lake, 15.

OPEN door, the, 113.
Orange River, 16.
Otterbein University, 189, 201, 204.
Our Martyred Friends (poem), 132.

PAGANISM, 29, 30.
Palli, revival at, 196.
Parent Board (see General Board of Missions).
Paris, conference at, 113.
Pa Sourri, 61, 195.
Pidgin-English, 53, 107.
Plantain Island, 125.
Poison, use of, 64.
Polygamy, 31, 56.
Population of Sierra Leone, 42.
Porroh, 67, 110, 122, 123.
Portugal, 22.
Priests, 29.
Property of Missions, 125.
Protectorate of Sierra Leone, 42, 122.
Protestant missionaries, number of, 36.

QUININE, 209.

RACES, 24.
Railroad, 122.
Rainfall, 16, 52.
Recollections of massacred missionaries, by Mrs. Lida M. West, 171.
Red pepper a preventive of fever, 71, 83.
Red Sea, 13.
Religious, 28.

Religious customs, 61.
Reptiles, 18.
Resurrection of body not known, 63.
Rotufunk, 43, 77, 137, 139, 150, 153, 156, 161, 181, 192.
    property at, 126, 127.
    revival at, 182, 195.
Rum, 32.
    international agreement as to, 33.
    Miss Williams stops the sale of, 193.

SABBATH services, 173, 226.
Sage, W. S., 238, 239.
Sage, Mrs. W. S., 238, 239.
Schenck, Miss Ella, 127, 156, 157, 160, 176, 178, 179, 202, 239.
    life of, 162.
Scorpion, 18.
Scriptures, translations of, 108.
Secret societies, 67.
Semites, 24.
Semitic languages, 26.
Separation of missionaries, 87.
Shaingay.
    at time of massacre, 124.
    schools at, 43.
    site of first United Brethren mission, 74.
    work at, 225, 226.
Sherbro-Mendi district, 81.
Sherbros, 47.
Shuey, W. J., 73, 230, 236.
Sick, the, abandoned, 96.
    incidents of, 97.
Sierra Leone, 37.
    animals, 40.
    Christians in, 42.
    colony, 43.
    domestic animals, 40.
    educational institutions, 43.

English claims to, 106.
flora, 41.
free negroes colonized there, 106.
peninsula of, 38.
population, 42, 106, 107.
tribes, 43.
wars, 127.
Slavery, 34.
   effect of on labor, 90.
   Livingstone on, 35.
Society, 51.
Somaliland, 20.
Sorcerers, 29, 62.
Soul, survival after death, 29, 63.
Sowers Home for Girls, 99.
   work of, 100.
Spain, 22.
"Spider, De," 109.
Stead, on England's possessions, 21.
Stealing, penalty for, 66.
Sudan, 16.
Sudanese, 24.
Suez Canal, 13.
Sunday school, 206.
   work in, 224.
Superstitions, 94.
Surgery, natives have no knowledge of, 71.
   surgical instruments, 159.
Susus, 48.
Swahili, 26.

TAIAMA, 137, 167.
Tanganyika, 15.
Temnis, 48, 123.
Termites, 18, 140.
Thomas, Lydia, 239.
Tigre language, 26.

Towns, 59.
Training school, 102.
Travel, mode of, 84.
Tsetse, 18.
Tucker, Thomas, first convert, 78.
Tugwell, Bishop, 118.

UNITED BRETHREN missions, among what tribes, 49
    extent of, 79.
      property at time of massacre, 126.
Uprising, causes of, 121.

VENEREAL diseases common, 71.
Verde, Cape, 14.
Victoria, Lake, 15.
Voices of natives poor, 71.

WAR, 32.
    implements of, 124.
Ward, Arthur A., 121, 127, 160, 240.
Warner, Peter, 237.
Warner, Mrs. Peter, 237.
West, Lida M., 163, 197, 239.
West, Richard N., 141, 177, 202, 238.
    work of in Africa, 180.
Western College, 142, 148, 151.
White ants, 140.
White population of Africa, 23.
    of Sierra Leone, 42.
Wilberforce, D. F., 124, 237.
Wilberforce, Mrs. D. F., 237.
Williams, J. A., 223.
Williams, Frances, 177, 239.
    death of, 209.
    funeral of, 216.
    life of, 186.

Wilson, C. O., 237.
Witchcraft, 64, 65, 94.
Witt, W. B., 74, 236.
Wolf, Joseph, 237.
Woman's Evangel, 182, 185, 188, 198.
Woman's Missionary Association, 155, 168, 181, 204.
    organized, 77.
    possessions and expenditures, 82.
    terms of service of missionaries, 236.
Work, mechanical, agricultural, and medical, 90.
    being done, 99.
Wundi Society, 69.
Wyandt, Baker, letter of, 220.

YATES and Porterfield, 46, 160.
Youra Bay, 125, 231.

ZAMBESI River, 15, 16.

www.ingramcontent.com/pod-product-compliance
Lightning Source LLC
Chambersburg PA
CBHW031330230426
43670CB00006B/295